Olive Champion was born ı _____ ᴸıverpool Ship-owning family. She worked aᴛ ᴃletchley during the 1939/45 War, and married John Champion, the son of a colonial Governor. Together they spent 17 years in Uganda and then, when he joined the F.C.O., she travelled with him to Iran and Jordan. In 1975 they were posted to the New Hebrides (now renamed Vanuatu) where he was the last but one British Resident Commissioner.

Olive now lives in South Herefordshire.

Olive and John – Above Manikarn in the Parbatti valley

Journey of A Lifetime

(1922 – 1993)

Olive Champion

A Square One Publication

First published in 1994 by
Square One Publications
Saga House, Sansome Place, Worcester, WR1 1UA

© Olive Champion 1994

British Library Cataloguing in Publication Data
is available for this book

ISBN 1: 1 872017 77 0

Typeset in Times 11 on 12 by Avon Dataset, Bidford-on-Avon,
Warwickshire B50 4JH
Printed by Antony Rowe Ltd, Chippenham, England

To John

CONTENTS

vii

Introduction

When I was a child and first starting to learn about dates and time I was excited to think that I might live to see the year 2,000 A.D. Later I thought that if I did I would then write the story of those years, but now that I am 70 it seems a good idea to do it now. After all I may not reach 2,000 A.D., and in any case the most interesting part of my life is probably now behind me.

It seems to me that life, both for the individual and the group is like a long journey uphill; our perspective changes as we go higher, and while individuals fall by the way and die the group goes on, so that all life is a continuous process. When we are young we are so busy and preoccupied by the present and the immediate future that the past is of almost no importance; as we grow older and the perspective lengthens we become more curious about what it was like in the hazy distance, but by then the people who could have told us are gone, and we shall never know. So, in the hope that it may interest and perhaps amuse my children and grandchildren, I am going to try to describe my journey through the twentieth century, troubled by wars and the dissolution of empires, and caught in an ever accelerating whirl of technology.

1. Origins

I was born in Liverpool on August 5, 1922. I remember nothing about this, needless to say, but I know that I was born in my parents' home, and to judge by what happened when my younger brothers Julian, David and Stopford, were born my mother, who was 22 while my father was nearly 40, will have had to stay in bed for a month afterwards. My father's family on both sides were classic examples of successful 19th century bourgeoisie. George Holt, my great-grandfather, whose own father was a mill-owner in Rochdale, came to Liverpool in 1805 with a guinea (£1.05p — worth a lot more in those days than now) in his pocket to work in a bank. He prospered, founded his own business, went in for cotton-broking and insurance, married into the Durnings, a well-off Liverpool family, and died in the 1860s, I think, leaving sons William, George, Alfred, Philip and Robert — and some daughters whose names I do not know. George was a successful businessman, collector and philanthropist; Alfred and Philip founded the Blue Funnel shipping line, and Robert went into the family cotton broking business. Robert was my grandfather, and also the first Lord Mayor of Liverpool. He died in 1910, having married Lawrencina Potter, who died in 1906. They had eight children, of whom my father, Lawrence Durning, born on November 27, 1882, was the youngest.

Lawrencina Potter was the eldest daughter of Richard Potter II, and one of the famous Potter sisters, of whom the formidable Beatrice Webb, my great-aunt, is the best known. Her father, Richard, had various business ventures, not all of them successful, including the promotion of the Canadian Pacific Railway, but to my mind it is his father, the first Richard Potter who is the more interesting. He was born in

1

the late 18th century to a farming, shop-owning family near Tadcaster. Two unmarried resolute sisters, Catherine and Elizabeth, managed the family. Young Richard was apprenticed to a shopkeeper in Birmingham at the time of the French Revolution. The sisters kept him hard at it; it was a hard life: all day in the shop, six days a week, church on Sunday mornings and only Sunday afternoons free. But somehow young Richard prospered; he learnt French, and acquired good radical opinions on the way. By 1830 he was active in the agitation on the Reform Bill, and involved in the founding of London University: in those days non-conformists were not allowed into Oxford or Cambridge. He had also married a Miss Mary Seddon. Family legend has it that she was a gypsy, hence the dark eyes and wayward behaviour of some of us, but I have no evidence of this. I think it is a bit of genealogy which should be treated with the same scepticism as that which should be applied to the tale of my husband's Macgregor ancestors in the Lairig Ghru (of which more later). John did not agree.

My mother's father, Lawrence Pearsall Jacks, LPJ to his family and friends, was born in 1861. His father, son of a parson, the Revd James Jacks, himself the son of a sailor, was a shopkeeper in Nottingham. Family legend traces descent to Huguenots in the Orkneys, but I treat this with the same reserve as I do the origins of the Macgregors. LPJ's father died in 1874, bankrupt and ruined, and his mother had a hard time to survive. However LPJ was clever and fortunate in his friends, who encouraged him to persevere with education — not at all easy to do in those days. After theological studies he visited America in 1886, meeting many theologians and philosophers, most of them Unitarians. While there he was invited to become assistant to the Revd Stopford Brooke at the Bedford Unitarian Chapel in London. He had also met in America two of Stopford Brooke's six daughters, who were travelling with their uncle, Major-General Edward Brooke, and came back to England with them on the *Pavonia*. By the time they reached England he was engaged to one of them, my grandmother, Olive.

The Brookes were a very different kind of family from the Holts, Potters or Jacks. Descended — and this is fairly

Olive – 1923

reliably authenticated — from a mistress of King Edward III, they were part of the Anglo-Irish establishment, and include some successful ruffians among them, such as Hector Graham of Leix Castle, who went over to Ulster from Netherby at the time of Elizabeth I. Later they became more civilised 18th century gentlemen and writers in Dublin. Stopford Brooke, starting off as a Church of England parson, married a Beaumont, sister, I believe of the first Earl of Allendale, by whom he had the six daughters referred to. She died young, and the daughters were brought up by their aunt, Cecilia. Stopford Brooke himself became a Unitarian, and was a poet, philosopher and author. He was a friend of William Morris.

When LPJ married Olive Brooke he became the Minister of Renshaw Street Unitarian Chapel in Liverpool, where the Holts were among the many rich and locally important members of his congregation. When LPJ's first child, a boy, died at six months, Lawrencina Holt was very kind to my other grandmother, Olive. My mother, the only girl in a family of six, was born on December 28, 1899. Meanwhile LPJ had moved first to Edgbaston in 1894, and then, in 1905 to Manchester College Oxford as professor, and in 1915 as Principal. The connection formed with the Holts was maintained, and later, when my cousin Anne, the daughter of my father's eldest brother, went to Oxford during the war, she used to visit the Jackses. In fact the 1914–1918 war brought prosperity to some people, including the Blue Funnel Line, and after the war, in 1919, my bachelor father celebrated with a great house-party lasting several weeks at Torosay on the Isle of Mull. He invited my Jacks grandmother to act as his hostess, and she took my mother, then 19, with her. That was how my mother met my father; they were married on October 10, 1920.

2. 52 Ullet Road
1922 – 1935

My great uncle Philip, towards the end of the 19th century, when the Blue Funnel Line was in its early flourishing years, built a substantial house at 52 Ullet Road on the edge of Sefton Park in Liverpool, next door to the rather similar home of his brother Robert at No 54, where my father was born. 54 still stands; it is now a nurses hone, but No 52 was handed back to the city council, which owned the lease, after the 1939 – 1945 war, and it was pulled down. Now there is a large bloc of ugly flats on the site. 54 looks rather sad beside it. 52 itself, as shown in the picture taken just before my family left it, was a solid, self-confident house, very appropriate for a successful Victorian businessman. Philip Holt died childless in 1915, and after the first world war my father moved in, and took my mother there when they married in 1920. During the 1914 – 1918 war taxation was not nearly so severe as it became later, and shipping, despite losses from the submarines, had been very profitable, so that my father was able to live with a certain style. There were two servants in the kitchen (Mrs Rees the cook and her helper), two parlourmaids (Mary and her under-parlourmaid), two housemaids (Annie and her under-housemaid), and later Nanny (Mrs Lyons) together with Agnes (and later Sarah) in the nursery. There was also a gardener (Disley) and his helper, and Leaf the chauffeur. My father had a splendid early convertible Rolls Royce, with a hood that could be raised and lowered, a large glass windscreen between the driver and the passengers, and an impressive boot. It was as long as a minibus. He loved this car, and kept it till 1936, by which time it was distinctly an oddity, and as such caused me much embarrassment with my schoolfellows. There was a

5

52 Ullet Road

large garden, mainly lawns and bushes, which Joined the garden of 54, where my uncle Dick (my father's eldest brother) and Aunt Eliza reigned. They had a butler and a footman. There was a certain amount of what I think is called sibling rivalry between the eldest and youngest brothers, and my mother, young and unsophisticated, accepted all my father's prejudices – which we children quickly acquired also. I regret this, as Uncle Dick and Aunt Eliza were constantly making friendly gestures, but were rebuffed : no childrens' parties were ever encouraged between the two families – a mistake. However we were able to play freely in both large gardens, and I remember the excitement of climbing a large mulberry tree in the garden of 54, and wondering if I would be caught.

My mother taught me to read, and then when I was five there appeared Miss Bloxham who taught me, my brother Julian and several other approved children until I was eight, when I went to the Liverpool College for Girls in Huyton as a day girl. Leaf drove me and three others every day to school in the Vauxhall, which was the second family car. I don't remember much about Huyton except that it was made very clear to me that I was no good at sewing, and not much good at drawing either. However I was clever, and by the time I was 11, I was in a class of 16 year olds due to take School Certificate (the equivalent of the now obsolete "O" level) that summer. My parents did not think that this was a good thing — and they were right. Also I had to be taught Latin and Greek properly. My father had been taken away from school at 16 and made to become an office boy. This was because two of his elder brothers who had gone to Oxford had misbehaved, and my grandparents were not going to have this happen again. A pity, as my father would have benefited from university in many ways. As it was, Oxford had for him the attraction of the unobtainable, and of course the classics were *the* subject to be studied there. So in 1934 I found myself sent to the Dragon School in Oxford. This famous boys Prep School was then prepared to take girls who had associations with it; as several of my mother's brothers had been there I was acceptable. I spent a happy year there duly learning Latin and Greek, maths, a little French, and not much else, playing hockey, canoeing on the Cher, having a famous fight with Corinna Blackwell (with boys putting bets on us), interrupted by the start of a lesson, and having my first boy-friend, Rupert Marshall. This episode lasted about a week, when pitiless teasing by the other boys — I couldn't think why – brought the affair to an end. Later Rupert was killed in a tank in the Western Desert.

My father was Lord Mayor of Liverpool from 1929 – 30. It was just before the financial collapse of 1931, and he made civic visits to Amsterdam and Hamburg in the hope of encouraging trade, goodwill and co-operation. I was too young to be aware of much of this, although when there were parties at the Town Hall my mother would come to say "Good Night" wearing new, and to me glamorous dresses, and there was an atmosphere of great activity. I do remember my mother coming back from Hamburg and talking of unemployment and poverty: ripe conditions for the growth of National Socialism — and also of the enormous meals she had had to eat.

3. Wales

During these years family holidays were taken in North Wales, and I acquired a lasting love for that beautiful and distinctive land. The early holidays were spent in Clynnog Fawr. When I went there again with the Cambrian Archaeological Association in 1979 I was pleasantly surprised how little it had changed. At first we stayed in the old schoolhouse, but then, as the family grew, we went to Bryn Eisteddfod on the opposite side of the road. A pony appeared called Wendy, who bit me in the stomach on one occasion, causing a great deal of yelling. We also bathed and played on the then empty beach, and I remember a journey in a donkey cart to fetch a sack of meal. This was exciting as by then the motor car had already taken over road transport, and it was a special treat, — especially the donkey part of it. My father encouraged us to go into the hills, and I remember the thrill of exploring old mine workings on Bwlch Mawr. During the winter holidays we went to Llanfairfechan, where we stayed in a boarding house called Garfield on the front, and there on winter mornings I would get up early, creep downstairs, steal chocolate biscuits, and go out and run along the sands watching the stars and feeling exalted. Would a child of eight be able to do that now?

Early in the 1930s our holidays became more ambitious. Winter was spent in Liverpool, with Sunday outings to the again empty beach at Formby, but in spring and summer we migrated in strength to Glasfryn in Eifionydd. This was, and still is, the home of the Williams Ellis family. The 1930s were hard times for landowners, and they were happy to let their house to us twice a year, and to stay somewhere in

Carmarthenshire I think. A large removal van would come to 52 at the beginning of the exodus, and take a lot of our equipment and also some of our staff down to Glasfryn, where we stayed for a month. Like many similar Welsh houses Glasfryn had been extensively re-built in the 19th century, but it had a panelled dining room of Stuart times, and many family portraits which interested my parvenue taste. And there were woods, miles of bog, hills and lanes to ride over, and no tractors, hedge-cutters, combine harvesters or fast motorbikes to terrify my pony. Also there was a lake with a boat in which we learnt to row, and I remember one occasion when Roger Williams Ellis, the present owner, and I pushed Julian out of the boat, and then beat his hands with our oars as he tried to climb in again. I can't remember what happened after, but obviously Julian survived.

The farm, of about 350 acres, was managed by Richard Thomas, a jovial character who got a great deal of fun in teasing us. One day he asked me if I would like to see a sheep being killed. "Oh Yes!" I said, thrilled, and watched the whole process with much interest. I will spare the squeamish reader all the details, but merely say that after I had told it all to my parents, ending up with: "And the dogs sat around with their tongues hanging out, and then they licked up the blood", I found myself discouraged from Richard Thomas' company in future. It was also about this time that my brother David and I tried to burn our youngest brother Stopford, then known as Tiny. He was about three at the time, and we thought dreadfully spoiled. So when mother had gone off to the wedding of an old friend, taking Julian with her to be a 'page', I said to David, "Let's teach Tiny a lesson". I had been busy reading Fox's Book of Martyrs and stories about Red Indians, so Tiny was tied to a tree and sticks and leaves were piled around him. Fortunately they were all very wet, so failed to light; Tiny's screams and yells brought help running, and he was released. When mother heard the story she behaved very sensibly: there were no excessive reproaches, but I remenber being made to sit on her knee — rather awkward for a solid girl of nine — and told that I could sit on her knee whenever I liked; she was as fond of me as of Tiny; but I might just find it a bit uncomfortable.

I saw the point, and felt no more need to teach Tiny lessons.

During these years too I first got to know Aunt Molly, who will always be remembered with immense affection by her nephews and nieces and cousins for as long as they survive. She was my father's youngest sister, and did not marry till her 50s; she was a wonderful aunt to all who were lucky enough to know her. At the time when I used to stay with her she had a house, Little Bryans Ground, outside Presteign, and a cottage in Radnorshire by Llyn Helyn. This was a real cottage: two rooms upstairs above the kitchen, which had an open fire; no electricity of course; an earth closet outside in what had been a cowshed; no running water — you fetched it from a spring piped beside the main road — a weekly bath in a tub by the fire; and on the outside miles of heather clad moor. I used to go there in September, after Glasfryn. Thinking back, it must have been splendid for my parents to have me occupied and out of the way for the rest of the holidays. It was blissful. I ran wild and free — it was a point of pride to be able to run barefoot down the track to the next gate without flinching. Bilberries and cranberries grew on the moor, and you could bathe in Llyn Helyn, which in those days was clear, with a hard bottom. Years later, in the 60s, I took my own children there and persuaded them of the delights of Llyn Helyn. But alas! the moor had been turned into pasture; cows roamed the shore of the lake, which had become a muddy midden. Sally went in protesting — but never again! Aunt Molly had several dogs, all well trained, but not, I suspect, very clean, because I remember going home each time with red, itchy spots which I was told were 'heat spots'. I believed this, and it wasn't till years later that I realised that of course they must have been flea bites.

Holidays at Glasfryn were spent exploring the woods and bogs, learning the names of birds and flowers, and in riding. There were two ponies, Lily and Polly, and later a cob called Tommy which my mother rode occasionally. But she never took to riding, so my father came out with us on him. Julian had a bad fall off Polly, and was never a keen rider, but David and I rode together until the war brought these pleasures to an end. It was before the days of Pony Clubs, so

I learned to ride, partly from a book called 'Moorland Mousie', and partly from experience; technique came much later. However I did win first prize in the Mountain Pony class one year at the Pwllheli Show. There were two entrants: myself on Lily, a pretty 12.2 chestnut, and the local butcher's boy on a similar sized blue roan. The competition consisted of a race which Lily won, round and round the ring to wild applause. So I received the coveted red 1st Prize ticket, while the butcher's boy had to make do with a blue 2nd Prize. Then we set off again on a lap of honour, round and round, until at a corner the band struck up; Lily swerved, and I flew off to even greater applause. I picked myself up a bit dazed, but nobody took away my prize, which was what mattered.

4. 1935 – 1940:
Growing up to the Rumble of Distant Guns

In the summer of 1935 I went to Wycombe Abbey School, where Latin and Greek were well taught, which was what mattered. I vaguely remenber taking the scholarship exam, and think I must have been successful. Wycombe was a rude shock after the freedom of the Dragon School. As anyone who has had the same experience will know, summer is not a good term in which to join a new school: everyone has already made friends and you are a conspicuous outsider. (Incidentally we inflicted the same unfortunate experience on our own David, 26 years later at Shrewsbury). In addition my background and upbringing, a mixture of wealth and idealism, was different from that of my fellows, and it takes skill and experience to fit yourself easily into strange surroundings. For instance my father disapproved of the corrupting influence of the cinema, so we never went. I read Fox's Book of Martyrs instead, and had never heard of Shirley Temple or any other important film stars. This marked me out as an oddity from the start. However I did eventually learn to get on with my fellows, and in retrospect Wycombe did as much for me as the Diplomatic Service much later in enabling me to accept and even to enjoy the company of people different from myself.

It was the rules and disciplines that I found most trying. Whatever my father's disapproval of the cinema, reading of all kinds had always been encouraged at home; at Wycombe there was a selected library for the under-16s; interesting books like 'Gone with the Wind' were reserved for the older girls. So I kept my own selection, French books like 'Le Dieu du Corps' and exciting ones like 'The Seven who Fled' by Frederic Prokosh, under a loose plank in the music practising block. I was discovered reading one of these during a boring Monday evening lecture and there was a lot of trouble. There were many similar incidents. I remember my parents being summoned on one occasion, and suspect that had I not been expected to get a scholarship to Oxford I would have been expelled. However I gradually came to terms with the system, and my last year, when I actually became a house monitor, was comparatively uneventful. And I duly did get a scholarship to Somerville in December 1939 to read Honour Moderations in Greek and Latin literature in the following year.

My parents had been justified in choosing Wycombe Abbey for its teaching. Not only were Latin and Greek well taught to a select few, but during the year between School and Higher Certificate (ie O and A levels), we were given a much wider and more varied choice of subjects than for example John was given at Shrewsbury. But above all I am grateful to one teacher, Miss Partridge. Sarcastic and ruthless (She would creep along at night listening for people talking after 'lights out', and then pounce), she was yet a brilliant teacher of Divinity. I rejected religion totally at the age of 13 as clearly a lot of sentimental, superstitious rubbish, used by authority to bully people who disagreed with them. However Divinity was a compulsory subject for School Certificate, and we were taught by Miss Partridge. She continued to teach us Comparative Religion the next year, and when I finally left school I was aware that there were more things in heaven and earth than I had dreamed of. Job was one of the books we had to study, and I do not know of a more satisfactory attempt to reconcile humans to their inescapable suffering.

While term followed term at school, holidays at Glasfryn continued, but in 1935 there was a change; in the summer we went to stay in Norway on the Oslo Fjord at a place called Tjömö, rather an attractive wooded island off the main coast. Here we bathed, went in a hired motor boat to the surrounding islands, and for the last two years my father hired a sailing boat as well. We fished off the rocks and learnt to dive, and even indulged in nude bathing, a Scandinavian specialty. It was on the journey to and from Newcastle that I became familiar with the joys of seasickness. My father had never been seasick, and was sure that fresh air and exercise provided a reliable cure, — but after many a vain walk around the deck I am quite sure that he was wrong. On our last journey back to Newcastle in August 1939 a German submarine surfaced near the Fred Olsen steamer in which we were travelling. There was great indignation among the Norwegian crew, and also head-shaking by my parents. By then war was considered almost inevitable.

Many books have been written describing the run-up to the 1939 – 45 war. I shall not attempt to do this, but shall try to describe how it appeared to me. It is important to remember the enormously traumatic effect of the 1914 – 18 war on public opinion, and particularly on enlightened, self-styled intellectual, or what might now be called 'politically correct,' opinion. It had been a war to end wars; the League of Nations was to prevent it happening again. It was not until the mid-1930s that it began to be recognised that it could do so again. Even then the Peace Pledge Union (a fore-runner of C.N.D.) was still fulminating; many a tedious sermon I endured at Wycombe; and advocates of re-armament were shunned as warmongers. Mussolini's invasion of Abyssinia in 1935 revealed the powerlessness of the League of Nations, the Spanish Civil War, and Hitler's annexation of Austria showed the growing strength of the Fascists, yet still appeasement seemed a practical policy. I remember listening with my parents on the radio (wireless as it was called then) to

Hitler speaking at the Nuremburg rally. I couldn't understand, but there was no mistaking the screeching, menacing note of hysteria. Years later, during the 1984 miners' strike I heard Dennis Skinner on the radio. There was the same shrieking tone of hysteria, and I felt a frisson; but fortunately Dennis Skinner is no Hitler, nor was Margaret Thatcher a Neville Chamberlain.

My father, who had vision, was well aware of what was happening. He knew how feeble our navy was, and he saw too our weakness in the Far East, which the Japs were able to,exploit in 1941. I remember at dinner in the evenings in Liverpool (a three course meal in the dining room, for which we had to change), listening to him inveighing against Baldwin and later Chamberlain, and some official called Sir Horace Wilson who seemed to be evil incarnate. So I knew, when Chamberlain brought back 'Peace with Honour' in 1938, after the betrayal of Czechoslovakia, that war was then inevitable, and I was not surprised when it broke out in September 1939.

5. Family and Friends

Before proceeding to Oxford and the war, it seems an appropriate moment to say something of family and friends, As I have said, my father had vision; he was also something of a romantic but stern idealist. However, as I am trying now to recall my own memories and experience, I shall only write of him as I knew him as a father, and not attempt to assess him as a businessman, local politician, or even as joint founder, with Kurt Hahn, of Outward Bound. Although he was well into his forties by the time my youngest brother was born, he was a jovial father, romping happily with us, and later teaching us to ride, walk on the hills, swim and enjoy cold bathing in the rough seas off Wales. During the thirties in Liverpool, long before the 5-day week, he would go to the office in Water Street on Saturday mornings, come home for lunch, and then set off in his old Rolls with me and one of my brothers or one of his walking friends, and drive down to Capel Curig, where we stayed in the Royal Hotel (now I believe a Youth Hostel), then on the Sunday, walk on the hills — Moel Siabod, the Glyders, the Snowdon circuit, and once the Carnedds — and drive back to Liverpool in the evening. My mother, who early gave up these expeditions, impressed on me, "Whatever happens you mustn't spoil your father's walk". So I learned never to complain even when my calf muscles were crying out in anguish. And so from my father I acquired my love of hills and mountains and of the wild places of this earth, and also my thick, solid calves, which have carried me to so many interesting places.

Of my father's family we saw quite a lot of Uncle Dick and Aunt Eliza next door: always friendly to us children, whatever adult tensions there may have been, and also of their unmarried daughter, Cousin Anne. She was my mother's age, clever and deaf. Hearing aids were then in their infancy. Hers was a small square box which she wore in her bosom. When bored with conversation she would reach in and switch it off; when faces around her became more animated she would switch on again and join in: rather a useful facility. The other Holt who featured largely in my childhood was Cousin Emma. She was the daughter of my father's uncle George, his only child, and lived in some splendour in Sudley on Mossley Hill. Before we were old enough to go down to Capel Curig on Sundays we used to walk up after Sunday dinner (invariably roast beef, potatoes, Yorkshire pudding and apple pie), to have tea with her. I remember an old lady with a black velvet band round her neck, in a large house with a lot of pictures, a marble bust in the hall, a musical box which gave birth to a white rabbit — and very dull teas: chocolate biscuits were not good for children. Sudley passed to the City Council, and is now being imaginatively restored by the Walker Art Gallery as a Victorian museum. I felt ashamed when asked by the Director a few years ago what I could remember of the furnishings, and could be of no more help to him than this.

My grandfather LPJ, described by Henry Fairlie a few years ago in an article I kept, but can no longer find, as "that curious figure to be found in Oxford in the 20s and 30s," can best be understood from his autobiography, 'Confession of an Octogenarian'. I remember him as white haired, congenial, and with a beautiful voice. We visited him and my grandmother fairly often in the houses LPJ built for himself on Shotover outside Oxford: first Shotover Edge, then Greatstones, and finally Far Outlook. Other Jacks relations were my Uncle Oliver and Aunt Alice, and Uncle Stopford and Aunt Kate — both families near Manchester; Uncle Maurice and Aunt Emma — he was Headmaster of Mill Hill; and also Uncles Graham and Hector, whom we saw less often. Maurice and Stopford had married sisters, daughters of the Greg family from Styal, famous as enlightened and successful 19th century millowners. I have memories of them all: affectionate and thoroughly amusing and agreeable.

Two of my father's friends impressed my youthful memory particularly. One was his boyhood friend, Harold Armstrong, Uncle Am as we knew him. He had the useful skill of being able to make glass fingerbowls sing, and also had funny stories about some of his aristocratic clients: he was a lawyer. The other was the Dean of Liverpool cathedral, F.W. Dwelly, Dean Dwelly as we knew him. Despite very opposing views on the subject of appeasement he and my father became firm friends, and he was often at 52 during the late 30s. There was a great clerical row, 'The Liverpool Cathedral Controversy' when he invited my heretical free-thinking grandfather LPJ to give a sermon in the cathedral. Dean Dwelly was very kind to us children, showing us round the new anglican cathedral then under construction, and also trying to interest me in the poetry of Robert Bridges, but I preferred Byron. One other person of whom we were all very fond was Françoise Renou. Her family and my father's family had long been friends; my father as a boy had visited her family near Tours, and I was to go there in 1946. Françoise came to us 'en famille' in the 30s to learn English and teach us French. I think she profited more than we did, though I do remember David and me chasing her round the house with laughing cries of 'Sale cochon', and being

16

severely reprimanded for this by my mother. Françoise went back to France in 1938, and married. Her family had more than their share of suffering during the war. Her elder sister, Solange, was a nurse, and died of septicaemia (no antibiotics then); Françoise died in childbirth fleeing from the invading Germans, and her older brother Jean was killed by the Royal Navy when they took out the French navy at Oran in North Africa. Only a younger boy, André, survived with Françoise's two children, Madeleine (I think) and 'le petit Gérard', who were brought up by their grandparents. Nonetheless her parents were very kind and welcoming to me when I stayed with them in Pérusson in 1946. I walked through the meadows with the children, borrowed 'la vieille bicyclette de Madame', and rode through still unspoilt Touraine, and gathered from conversation with Monsieur that 'la Résistance' were a bunch of murderous thugs and not the heroic freedom fighters that I had supposed. I also learned that to the French the battle of Poitiers was when Charles Martel defeated the Arab invaders, and had nothing to do with the Black Prince.

Amongst family visitors, although only remotely connected, I must mention Harry Allen from New Zealand. His Aunt had married my father's brother, Uncle Ted, who emigrated to N.Z. in the early 1900s. My father had many stories of adventures in the bush there with Ted, some of which my mother used to stop so that we never heard the outcome. Harry came to Liverpool in the mid-1930s to join the 'Conway' training ship in the Mersey, and later to go to sea with the Blue Funnel Line. He spent his holidays with us. A few years older than I was, he was to my mind glamorous and dashing, and at the age of 15 I boosted my self-esteem at school with imaginary, and totally untrue accounts of what I think would now be called our 'relationship'. In about 1938 Harry found the air more to his liking than the sea, and joined the RAF. He was one of the early Spitfire pilots, and was shot down over the sea during the Battle of Britain.

Finally there was my mother's friend Rita Guthrie. Her husband Frank was a professor at Liverpool University. He remains rather a shadowy figure, but I well remember Rita and their two sons, Bob and Ted, with whom we used to go

17

to the beach at Formby for picnics. Later, when I was getting married and John's parents were in Aden, she had John and his 15 year old brother Tony, his best man (Wallis Hunt, a fellow subaltern, having been unable to get leave for the occasion due to the imminence of the invasion of Normandy), to stay for the night before the wedding. I gather John filled in the time by playing Handel's 'Dead March in Saul' on their piano. It is an interesting illustration of the close social groupings of those days that about that time we discovered that a Stevenson relation of John's had married a Guthrie, and that Rita was a friend also of John's mother and grandmother. This all helped to make John's otherwise unknown background acceptable to my parents.

6. Pencraig and Oxford
September 1939 — May 1943

It was in 1938 that my father bought Pencraig. By then he was certain that there would be war; air raids were likely, and he wanted somewhere the children could be sent to be safe and also out of the way, leaving him undistracted to devote himself to the care of his ships and his crews. 52 became the Blue Funnel office when India Buildings in Liverpool were bombed in 1941.

Pencraig, with two downstairs rooms, a large kitchen and larder, four upstairs bedrooms and an attic, is a typical Welsh farmhouse between Pencaenewydd and Llanarmon, just north of the B4354 a few miles from Pwllheli. It had a walled garden and orchard, traditional Welsh farm buildings, and about 12 acres of land. When we came back from Norway in August 1939 my mother and the children went down to Pencraig and my father followed. The morning of September 3rd was grey and drizzly, but we never worried about the weather and David and I went down on our

Pencraig

bicycles to bathe at Abererch beach. When we came back war
had been declared. The adults were gloomy but I, aged 17,
was excited. However nothing much seemed to happen; a few
ships were sunk; Poland was invaded and divided between
Russia and Germany; children were evacuated from the
major towns (many of them later went home); and I went
back to Wycombe for my last term and the scholarship to
Oxford. From then on, until 1946, Pencraig was home.

My mother found herself, not entirely I suspect of her own
choice, living entirely in Welsh-speaking Wales, house-
keeping, gardening, which she liked, and managing the
12 acre farm. All land was compulsorily controlled by the
War Agricultural Committee, and incomprehensible forms
had to be filled in and sent back at intervals. She was much
helped by a local farmer from Pencaenewydd, Mr. Watkins,
Watters as we called him, who became a firm friend and a
tower of strength. First Robert Jones who lived at Lletty

19

Wyn down the lane, then Evan Williams, and finally William Francis ran the farm and did the work. We kept two cows which calved at intervals, a pig, hens, ducks and turkeys, and we fattened young bullocks for market. We made hay for feed, and also grew oats which were thrashed on the place and used for poultry feed. Needless to say there were also two ponies, Pip and GPB (Gentlemen Prefer Blondes — my mare), and Tommy who did the farm work as well as pulling the trap which we acquired and used for shopping expeditions into Pwllheli. During term time the ponies were turned out on a moor beyond Four Crosses, where they ran wild but didn't seem to come to any harm. Catching them, however, often took some time.

My time at Pencraig was for me among the best days of my early life. Everything that I liked was there in Wales: hills and mountains, riding, and above all freedom. I would ride my bicycle to the Pennant valley, leave the bicycle, spend the day walking, and come back in the evening too tired to talk, and sometimes too tired to eat. My mother had to put up with a great deal, and I admire her for it. During all those walks I seldom saw anyone, and although my mother must have had many anxieties I don't think I was ever at risk from human violence, though when I remember scrambling over Crib Goch in a cotton skirt and gym shoes I realise how lucky I was never to have had an accident.

While life at Pencraig continued the war also took its course. The 1940 invasions, first of Denmark and Norway, and then of the Low Countries and France, caused great adult gloom, but again I found it all exciting. During the whole of the war my father never took a holiday, but he did come down to Pencraig every weekend, arriving at Chwilog by the last train on Friday and leaving by the first on Monday morning. So we heard at weekends of sunken ships, air-raids and disasters. However none of this bothered me. After all we had always won wars in the end, so of course we would win this one. And so we did, but not greatly to our advantage. After the Dunkirk débacle there was talk of a possible invasion of Britain, and in about July 1940 my parents began to discuss the possibility of sending us to a cousin of LPJ's in Canada. I was furious; already I saw myself as a heroic guerrilla fighter. However the sinking in August, with great loss of life, of a ship carrying child evacuees to Canada, put an end to that idea.

It was during this period that my father and Kurt Hahn, the headmaster of Gordonstoun, whose interesting history I am not qualified to tell as I don't remember it, though I do know that he had been a refugee from Germany, conceived the idea of Outward Bound. It was prompted to my father's mind by the great and unnecessary loss of life in the boats of torpedoed ships often caused by twentieth century urban ignorance and inability to cope with primitive conditions and hardship. Outward Bound was to provide an antidote to this. A trial course was started at Llandinam in I think 1941. My brothers Julian and David were sent along: they called it 'Hahn's Hell'.

One person I remember vividly from those days was Alfreda Humphreys, 'The Hump' as we called her. Unmarried, the last survivor of an old Welsh family, she lived in Plas Hendre by Abererch with two large Alsatians, which were fed on nettles, and a companion, Katie Roberts, who ran the house. Hendre was a beautiful and romantic place. An early 19th century gentry house, it was surrounded by woods and an overgrown wilderness of a garden full of interesting trees and plants, and some wonderful old-fashioned apple trees. The roof leaked and the outbuildings were in ruins, but inside it was warm and welcoming. I used to ride down on GPB, leave her in a tumbling stable, and then sit to eat a huge tea with delicious Welsh cakes, honey and home-made jam by the fire in the sitting room. The logs which fed the fire were uncut and too long and stuck out across the room, being pushed further into the fire as they were consumed. Then I would collect GPB and ride home through the winter night. The Hump was impervious to discomfort. I have watched admiringly as she ran barelegged through tall nettles pursuing a wayward hen. However there was one occasion when she showed, for a countrywoman, a curious lack of savoir faire. She hatched out some ducks from eggs which we had given her. Unfortunately there were nine drakes and only one duck , which she called Ermintrude. After a few months she rang up to say that she was worried by Ermintrude: all the feathers had come off her back and she had developed persecution mania. I took five ducks down in a box and brought five drakes back, and Ermintrude recovered.

7. Oxford, 1940 – 43

In October 1940 I went up to Somerville to read classics. The Battle of Britain was by then largely over, and thanks to the courage and skill of our fighter pilots the threat of invasion had been removed, although it was some time before this was generally realised. However apart from the occasional thudding sound of distant air raids, or the glow in the sky when bombers were over London or Coventry, life in Oxford was unaffected. I had a room with a coal fire, and half a bucket of coal provided daily — enough to ward off hypothermia but not enough to keep warm. However I solved this problem by sharing with my neighbour Rosemary Dawe; as a result we were both comfortably snug and became good friends. There were plenty of young women in Oxford, but the young men were not so numerous, although they were allowed to come up for a year's shortened course before being called up for military service. One young man from Shrewsbury School called John Champion had come up to Balliol with an exhibition to read classics under this arrangement, and we met for the first time at a lecture in Magdalen by Professor Hardy on the 'Influence of the Digamma on Homeric Metre'. For those who do not know I must inform you that the Digamma, an imaginary ancient Greek letter, did not actually exist, but the experts thought that it should have done to explain certain obscure anomalies in the metre of Homer's epic poems.

John and I found all this rather bewildering, not to say boring, and distracted ourselves during the lecture by playing first noughts and crosses, and then the game of completing squares. We attended only the first three of these weekly lectures, and I am afraid I can provide no further information on tha Digamma. Other lectures were more rewarding. I had the good fortune to hear Cyril Bailey talking absorbingly on Lucretius, and later Professor Frankel, with whom I studied the Agamemnon, roused my interest in ancient manuscripts, and showed me several which gave me an idea of what textual criticism was all about. My tutor at Somerville was Mildred Hartley, whom I found friendly, demanding when necessary, and always encouraging. She persuaded me to learn Latin Verse, not very successfully I'm afraid. It is a disappointment to me that though I can appreciate other peoples' verses I am quite incapable of even producing a limerick of my own, and I only achieved a $\beta -$ for Latin Verse. However in due course — in March 1942 — I sat for Honour Moderations and got a First. I was particularly pleased with getting an $\alpha -$ in the paper on Art and Literature which I had swotted up intensely during the week before the exams, supplemented by a visit to the Ashmolean museum. Do not ask me anything about it now.

Meanwhile John Champion and I had been pursuing our friendship, to the detriment I am afraid of his studies, although he also had to put in a full day's military training every week, and rowed for his College and sang in the Bach choir; it was not entirely my fault that he didn't get his First, and I like to think it was all worth it to him in the long run. His father, the grandson of a Kentish fruitfarmer, was a colonial administrative officer in Palestine, where John had been born; his mother, the daughter of the Very Revd Dr W.M. Macgregor, Principal of the Presbyterian Theological College in Glasgow and a former Moderator, was at that time in England waiting for an opportunity to rejoin her husband in Nazareth. His uncle, Duncan Macgregor, who had recently died had been a Don and tutor in ancient history at Balliol. A romantic, it was he who had relayed to John the legend of the Macgregors' origins in the Cairngorms. On the banks of a stream running down from the Lairig Ghru are the remains of some stone sheilings which, according to the Macgregor tradition, were the homes of a sept of Macgregor outlaws in the 16th century, who were hired by the rich Grants of Speyside to guard the pass for them against sheepstealing raiders, Mackenzies and the like, from the other side. These, John firmly believed, were his Macgregor forbears. A romantic tale, but apart from hearsay there is nothing to link the outlaws with his earliest recorded Macgregor ancestor, an honest miller in Dunkeld and progenitor of a long line of Presbyterian ministers; so I remain sceptical of the family descent in the absence of more concrete evidence.

John took his shortened Honour Mods. exam in the summer of 1942, and got a good Second. He then spent some months awaiting call-up and living in digs in Walton Street — very convenient for Somerville. When he was called up he was first sent to Perham Down and later to OCTU at Sandhurst. In those days students at Somerville were not allowed away from Oxford without permission, so in order to visit him I would climb over the bicycle sheds and jump down into the Radcliffe passage and catch a train to Andover or Camberley, feeling pleasantly daring in the process.

In the summer of 1942 I came back to Somerville to read for Greats, ie Litterae Humaniores — Ancient History and Philosophy: la Crême de la Creme. This was not a success. It is a common failing to blame others for one's own weaknesses, and knowing this I will say at once that I know that had I completed the course I would not have got a First. To begin with I found the history to be studied dull. I was very interested in the late Roman Empire, perhaps through similarities to our own times, but I found the Athenian Constitution deadly boring. Then there was philosophy, and here I think I am justified in criticising Oxford. In my ignorance and naiveté I had supposed Philosophy to be concerned with τό ότωσ όν, ie the reality of Being; when I went to tutorials with the Principal of Hertford it seemed to be concerned with quibbling over the meaning of words: very disappointing. My complaint is that before starting Greats I should have been given a reading list giving some idea of what was involved. However, whatever the excuses I soon became bored and restless. Also life at Oxford seemed increasingly irrelevant to what was going on elsewhere, and when in the autumn of 1942 conscription for women was introduced I welcomed the opportunity to escape. When he realised that I wasn't going to go on at Oxford my father pulled some strings. I remember vaguely an interview with Stafford Cripps the Cabinet Minister, my father's first cousin, and then another interview in a London office with a lot of people round a large mahogany table, at which I was asked if I had any special qualifications. Well, during the last few months at Oxford I had been having independent Persian lessons with a retired professor. Persia was one of the romantic fancies (associated with Flecker's Golden Road to Samarkand) that had usurped the place of Solon's Athens in my mind, so I said, "Yes, I speak a little Persian". A few weeks later I found myself in Bletchley!

Meanwhile John had been commissioned into the 11th Hussars (Prince Albert's Own), an armoured car reconnaissance regiment operating in the Western Desert. They were known as the Cherrypickers following a disgraceful episode in a cherry orchard during the Peninsular War — involving some nuns, I think. The officers wore dark cherry coloured trousers with their service dress in imitation of some rather gorgeous German Hussars with whom they had escorted Prince Albert from Dover to London on his way to marry Queen Victoria. In any case on 23 October 1942 John sailed off to join his regiment with the Desert Rats.

8. Bletchley
May 1943 — August 1945

When I joined the staff of Bletchley Park as an ATS corporal in May 1943 I was made to sign a piece of paper acknowledging that if I ever spoke to anyone about my work I would make myself liable to a minimum of 10 years in prison. This made a considerable impression on me, and so, when the story of the breaking of the German Enigma cypher began to be revealed in the 1960s, I felt rathered confused. Plenty has now been written about the work of the brilliant teams of decoders at Bletchley Park. What I am going to try to describe is how it was at the lower levels. There were army, navy and RAF sections, and a civilian one, mainly attached to the army. In order to emphasise the responsibility of our position, all other ranks, however unimportant, were given NCO status. Others rose to become sergeants; I remained a corporal all the time I was there except for ten days, after which I lost my new sergeant's stripe for leaving work 20 minutes early in order to catch the best train to North Wales for 48 hours leave. I did not mind: being a corporal gave me much more freedom off duty, which was what I wanted.

On joining up at the end of April 1943 I was first sent to an ATS training centre at Northampton for two weeks initiation into service life. I rather enjoyed this: we were a mixed lot, all very friendly, several illiterates but mainly good working class. I remember being surprised at how many of these, to me, tough young women cried for their Mums in bed at night. Wycombe had cured me of that. We were issued with our uniforms, and gas masks in convenient haversacks which were seldom used for carrying gas masks. The gas threat never materialised. The early ATS skirt was a khaki serge object with two seams down the sides, a ridiculous garment allowing no freedom of movement at all. Later a more sensible version was provided with two front pleats. I joined at the time of the changeover, and was issued with one of each. On the train journey from Northampton to Bletchley I threw the least acceptable one out of the train window. On arrival at Bletchley and kit inspection I said I had unaccountably lost it. Authority was not best pleased, and I found myself on a charge under Section 40 of the Army Act, for "Conduct prejudicial to good order and military discipline, in that while on active service she did by neglect lose a skirt". Hard words were spoken, but I got a new skirt of the right kind, which was what mattered,

At first there was no accommodation at Bletchley for all the staff, and we were billeted in the surrounding area. I was with the Barnes family in Bedford: Eric, a foreman at the

Vauxhall factory, Maud his wife, and Stan their 16 year old son, an apprentice at Vauxhall. During the six months I was there they were enormously kind to me, feeding me splendidly despite rationing, and putting up with my wandering habits. I left by the early train for Bletchley in the mornings and came back about 6pm. There would be a good meal, and then in the summer I would go off on my bicycle to explore the surrounding country — not at all like it is now, coming back at dark to another meal. I remember excellent syrup tart. I stayed with the Barnes family until January 1944, by which time Shenley Road Military Camp had been built in what was then open country outside Bletchley, and we were installed there.

For obvious security reasons we were not allowed to know of the work of any section except our own, and only those who were working for the Enigma team 'E' knew the great secret. Other decoders were known as 'F', and we in 'E' knew of their inferiority, or rather of our own superiority. This was reflected in the sort of persons chosen to work at junior level in the various sections. All the workers in 'E' were either intellectuals, like myself, or else the daughters of senior service officers; workers in 'F' came from more humble backgrounds, eg state secondary schools. Why intellectuals should have been considered particularly reliable is a mystery in the light of susbsequent revelations, but in the case of 'E' the judgement was correct. Workers in 'E' and 'F' all lived together quite harmoniously in army huts. I think I was in Hut 6. Socially there were definite distinguishing features: all the people in 'F' were exceedingly clean, continually washing their hair; the officers' daughters hardly washed at all, but always managed to look smart, while the intellectuals didn't wash either, and looked like it.

I will now try to describe my work. I was allotted to the section of 'E' which dealt with intercepted wireless messages from German airforce stations. The actual messages were deciphered by officers using the Enigma machine, and each officer studied his or her own special group. We received the undeciphered messages, and from them had to draw plans of the particular group we were observing. Every German station had its own distinctive call-sign, and we had to keep records of the number of messages from each, and their length. There were certain prefixes that also had to be noted. Thus priority airforce messages started KR. I have forgotten what that stood for, but priority army messages started SSD: *Sehr Sehr Dringend.* At first it was all quite interesting; for example, at the time when our bombers more or less destroyed Hamburg one could tell from the number of intercepted priority messages that something was going on. But after a time it became tedious, and anyway it was not what I had had in mind when I started to learn Persian. Bletchley was not Samarkand.

At about the time I moved to Shenley Road Military Camp, John's regiment was brought home from Italy as part of the 7th Armoured Division to prepare for the invasion of Europe, and found themselves in camp at Ashridge, only a few miles from Bletchley. We took up our meetings again, and after some uncertainty decided to get married, if possible before D-day. We made this decision in a tube train on the Northern Line, and John tore some webbing off my useful gas mask haversack, and tied it round my finger. Then we telephoned Liverpool from a call box in Waterloo station. When my father answered I asked for mother and got the reply, "Your mother's just had all her teeth out; she's lying down". So as we could do nothing about it ourselves my poor mother had to make all the arrangements for us herself, on top of this unexpected surprise: as a result of our hesitations she had just decided that we weren't going to get married after all, and had gone ahead with what I think is known as a 'clearance'. However she managed very well, and we were married on April 5th 1944 in Ullet Road Unitarian Church, down the road from 52. It rained on the day, but not very heavily. The church was packed with Holt family and friends. John was supported only by Rita Guthrie and his 15 year old brother Tony as his best man, since both his parents and his sister were by now in Aden. I remember very little of what went on; afterwards the guests had a slap-up lunch largely provided by Blue Funnel catering, while John and I were given sandwiches and put on a train for Grasmere, where we spent our two weeks honeymoon in the Dale Lodge Hotel (temperance, but there was a pub opposite). The previous occupant of our room had been the Archbishop of Canterbury. We took with us a tier of our wedding cake, which we kept on top of the cupboard and cut with John's steel army comb. We had some fine walking on our honeymoon, and one day walked over to Coniston for tea with Cousin Emma, by now very old and living in Tent Lodge by the lake shore. Years later, in the 80s, we revisited Grasmere; our honeymoon hotel had become a Retirement Home.

The allied invasion of Europe took place six weeks after the end of our honeymoon. John and his regiment landed in Normandy on D + 3. Life at Bletchley continued as before. I paid as little attention as possible to radio news and reports; already I realised I would hear little of importance in them. John wrote as often as he could, and I took life as it came, day by day, with long bicycle rides as an escape. About mid-August I went into my hut, to see a telegram on my bed. In the war a telegram meant bad news. Silence fell in the hut as I picked it up, and took it to the latrines to read. I opened it with a deep breath and firm resolution; it was rather confusing to see that it came from Aden, and said, "No word from John for 4 months is he all right?" I duly wrote back and said that as far as I knew he was. A few weeks later another telegram arrived. This time I was sure it must be IT, so I took it away again, only to find that it was from my brother David who was by then in the Navy, asking me to meet him in London. Later, when John came on leave and told me his experiences I found out that whenever I had worried about him he had been miles from the fighting, but that when I had thought he was safe he had actually been very much the opposite. So I learnt to pay even less attention to what was reported in the news.

As far as I remember the summer of 1944 was hot and sunny, and this had one rather amusing consequence. When Normandy was invaded the Fench farmers there found their normal markets cut off, but quickly acquired an unexpected new one. The makers of Camembert cheese persuaded the British troops that they had on offer an ideal present to send by the Field Post Office to their deprived families at home. As a result Mount Pleasant Post Office in London was said to be overflowing with leaking packages of overripe cheese with illegible addresses. One package duly arrived at Shenley Road Military Camp. Fortunately John had had the good sense to buy unripe cheeses, so when my dozen half-kilos arrived in Hut 6 they were just *à point*, and already smelling nice and interesting. I kept them beside my bed, and my friend Liz Greaves and I ate one a day, sitting outside in the sun (We later came out in large itchy spots as a result). By the end the Camembert had become almost liquid, and smelt strongly even for me. Anyone who is interested in the oddities of English class attitudes will not be surprised to learn that while the intellectuals and officers' daughters were unconcerned about this, the girls in 'F' section objected very much indeed, and I had to keep a low profile for some time afterwards.

It was during this time that I made two of my finest expeditions. At the end of September 1944, at the time of the abortive assault on Arnhem by our paratroops, I had 48 hours leave, to return to the evening shift (1600hrs to midnight) on the third day. I hitch hiked down the A5 to London, took the night train to Fishguard, changed at Carmarthen, and went by train to Tregaron. There I left the train and walked along what is now the road to Abergweswyn, then a metalled track, over the empty unforested hills, down and then up and across to a pool above the Claerwen dam. I was rather proud of finding my way with only a blue ½-inch Bartholemew's map. Luckily the weather was fine. Then I got lost, went down into the wrong valley, and there met a shepherd who directed me, saying at the end, "Mind you, you'll find it a bit rough like". And so I did, stumbling over tussocks and falling into bogs at the end of a long day. For rations I had some cheese, chocolate and apples. Finally I came down to the road over the main Elan dam, and there I met a farmer in a van who took me through Rhayader along the A44 for a few miles. By now it was nearly dark. I tried to shelter in a friendly barn, but furious dog barkings drove me off, and at last I slept in some bracken on a hillside to the north of the road, rather inadequately wrapped up in my groundsheet. Needless to say I was awake by dawn, and starting a long trudge along the

A44. Just as I was beginning to climb up to the Radnor Forest I was overtaken by a cattle truck, which took me to Kington. There I got a bus to Hereford, and when I got down at the station my feet were so sore that I nearly fell over. However I got a train to Oxford, where I spent the night in the YWCA, and so back to Bletchley the next day, feeling triumphant.

Towards the end of the war in Europe I had another walk worth remembering. I went by train to Hereford, spent the night in the YWCA in St Owen Street, hitch hiked to Hay, and then walked up what is now a popular tourist route, but then an unmetalled track, and on to Hay Bluff. As I was going up the Bluff I was seen by a man in a field, who started to pursue me, but I was young and fit and easily outdistanced him. My aim had been to walk along the entire ridge of the Black Mountain, but in those days there was no path — let alone the horrible, muddy over-trodden trail that is now part of the Offa's Dyke Path. So after a while I became tired with struggling through the heather, and I went down to Capel y Ffin, and walked along the track, which soon began to seem unending. Finally at dusk I found myself on the A465 by Pandy, hoping for a lift into Hereford. But none came, and at last I went to the little station. There were no trains due, but the very kind stationmaster stopped a goods train and put me on the engine. So I had the great experience of journeying on the footplate of a steam engine as far as where Sainsbury's now have their Hereford supermarket (it was then the goods yard), and of being deeply impressed by the strength of the man who stoked the fire — a mere lad as I remember.

31

9. Towards Another Country:
May 1945 — December 1946

The war in Europe came to an end in early May, and the war against Japan towards the end of August. I saw the news of the bombing of Hiroshima at a station on my way from Bletchley to stay in Dewsbury with Liz Greaves. Hardened though I was by then to tales of destruction I do remember a peculiar sense of horror, but I put it from me. What could I do? In any case it brought the war to an end, and saved the life of our later friend Charles Fulford-Williams, who would not have survived another winter as a POW in Japan. It also brought home John's indomitable Aunt Bo Macgregor, previously headmistress of a Church of Scotland girls school in Mukden in Manchuria. She was interned in a camp just outside Nagasaki when the second bomb was dropped. According to her story she had been collecting firewood when an enormous explosion flung her to the ground, and shrivelled the leaves of the tree above her. She must have been sheltered by the lie of the ground from the direct blast, and from fallout by the direction of the wind, for she returned safe and sound to her native Glasgow, and lived to be 99.

I left Bletchley early in September and returned to Pencraig. Meanwhile John was with the British forces occupying Berlin, and wondering how to get out of the army, and what to do next. In order to avoid the confusion and unemployment which had followed mass demobilisation after the end of the 1914 – 1918 war, a strict system of first in first out was being operated, but there were exemptions, eg for coal miners, and potential overseas and colonial civil servants. Partly, but not wholly, for this reason, although he had not long before been offered a job with Ocean

Steamships by my father, John decided to follow his own father into the Colonial Service. He came on leave for his interviews in the autumn. was accepted, and demobilised in January 1946, when he came to join me in Pencraig to await the chance of a passage to East Africa.

My family were totally lacking in any technical skills: to change the plug of an electric iron was an achievement; so when John built a very effective fruit cage, and then installed electric light in the farm buildings his reputation with the Holts soared. About a year later an inspector from the North Wales Electricity Board made some very disparaging comments about this installation, but by then we were both in Uganda. John always thought he was jealous.

We stayed in Pencraig until the end of May, when John left for Uganda on an aircraft carrier adapted as a trooper, *HMS Fencer*, with 400 civilians going to East Africa (including 90 White Fathers), and 600 naval ratings bound for Hong Kong, all in three-tier bunks in the aircraft hangar. Before he left we had had two holidays, one in early March to Humshaugh in Northumberland. I remember long walks over moors, and also a visit to the Sneep, then occupied by the Thompson family. One of John's grandmother's sisters, Aunt Do, had married a Northumberland farmer of that name near Bellingham. Now the Sneep belongs to the Macgregor family. We also went to Scotland to stay with my Aunt Eliza at Nethybridge. Uncle Dick had died in 1941, and she had retired there, not far from Rothiemurchus where they had long had a shooting lodge. The weather was fine and we walked on the Cairngorms where John used to spend his holidays as a boy, investigating the Macgregor legend. I hope we didn't shock Aunt Eliza (or her housemaid who unpacked our one small suitcase) too much with our unconventional behaviour: we came with virtually no change of clothes — emphatically none in which to dress for dinner.

There were enormous transport difficulties in the aftermath of the war, and in any case new recruits to the Colonial Service were not allowed to bring out their wives for the first six months after their arrival, so that they should not be distracted from learning the local language and studying for their magistrates law exam. So I had to stay behind until

December, and without the help of the Blue Funnel Line, and John's father, who was by then the Governor of Aden, I should have had to wait longer still. It was during this time, in September I think, that I went to stay with the Renou family, first for a fortnight in Pérusson near Tours, and then for two weeks in their appartement in Paris. I remember tobacco plants growing in the fields of Touraine and their distinctive strong smell, and I remember going to Loches to see the castle: no tourists, romantic and overgrown, and exciting because of the horrid tales of past cruelties. Paris was sunny, dilapidated and quiet. I wandered along the banks of the Seine, visited Notre Dame and various parks in a relaxed way untroubled by traffic. When I was there next, in 1990, I hardly dared cross a main road, such were the numbers, speed and ruthlessness of the whizzing vehicles.

Early in November I embarked at Birkenhead on the *Teucer* (Captain Bonham), an ancient Blue Funnel cargo ship on her way to the Far East. There were no other passengers; I shared the captain's bathroom, and ate with the ship's officers. As deck passengers there were four racehorses on their way to Singapore. Feeding them and mucking out was the job of the midshipmen. I remember wondering how easy they would be to handle after six weeks in a crate, but while I was on board there were no accidents. Until Gibraltar I was seasick; I don't remember anything about the voyage through the Med., but from Port Said on it was a delight. November is a pleasant time in the Red Sea, calm, fine and not too hot. I was allowed onto the bridge at night and to watch the wonderful tropical skies, my pleasure heightened by a considerable amount of gin consumed with the captain. Jedda was our first port of call, and we were there for ten days. Whatever it is now, then it had no harbour, and ships lay off the shore and unloaded into barges. The Blue Funnel agent there was a Dutchman who had ostensibly converted to Islam. However when he came on board, suitably dressed in full Arab clothing, and was safely installed in the captain's cabin, his first words were: "And now, where is the gin?" I made several trips ashore under his guidance. Aramco were already at work, and the first high-rise blocks were up, but most of the old Arab town still survived. I expect it's all gone now. Two British destroyers came in when we were there, and there was a party on board of one of them, where I met H. St J. Philby, the famous traveller and father of Kim Philby, the infamous traitor and spy.

We reached Aden towards the end of November, and I spent about two weeks there with John's parents. There were trips into the desert and up into the valleys of Shum Shum (the barren rocky mountain of Aden) with John's sister Liz, riding out at Khormaksar where there was a club, and in the evenings I remember sitting under the stars outside on the terrace of Government House, on the promontory at the entrance to the harbour, watching the ships coming into port. After two weeks or so a place was found for me on a RAF Dakota going to Nairobi via Hargeisa in Somaliland. There were no seats. only metal strips along the sides on which you sat; it was very noisy and very uncomfortable but at least I wasn't sick, unlike a senior brigadier, known as 'Slasher' Brown, who spent most of the time lying on the floor groaning, much to my concealed amusement. We reached Nairobi in the afternoon, and there, greatly to my pleasure and relief, was John to meet me. He had driven, not without incident when the clutch pedal had come adrift, in an ancient Studebaker which he had been able to buy at a sale of surplus Government vehicles, from Mbale, the District in Uganda just over the Kenya border where he had been stationed.

We spent the night in the Avenue Hotel, and next day set off on the rough 300 mile drive to Uganda — but not before an amusing encounter with Customs. I had been given a case of whisky as a farewell present by the *Teucer*. Whisky in East Africa was then in very short supply and strictly rationed, so the customs officer refused to let me take it in. After ineffectual protests John and I went to see his boss; we said that we had done nothing wrong: we hadn't attempted to conceal it, and if it was to be taken away from us someone should have to pay for it.

This presented bureaucratic difficulties; there were no precedents. Eventually the reply was, "Oh for God's sake, take it", so we did. The first night we spent at the Highland Hotel at Molo, at 9,000 ft. There was a fire in our room and the air was like wine; there was a smell of pine trees. The

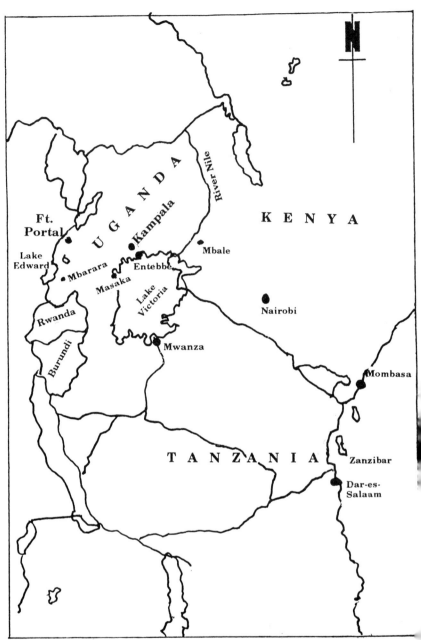

EAST AFRICA

whole wonderful country was immensely exciting; I was filled with happiness. The next day was rather different. As we rattled on our way towards the border one of the track rods on the old car snapped, and we found that progress was only possible if we restricted our speed to under 5mph. This happened just as children were coming out of the local schools; enthusiastic little boys insisted on being helpful and pushing us beyond the critical speed, and so off the road. However after an hour or two, when we reached the next little township a jovial Sikh was able to tie the loose ends of the track rod together with a piece of rope. The effect of this was to enable us to proceed at nearly 20mph, and we finally reached home in Mbale about midnight.

10. Uganda, Mbale — Mbarara
Dec. 1946 — July 1948

Uganda in 1946 was a British Protectorate. There were four Provinces: Northern, Western and Eastern, each with a Provincial Commissioner, based respectively at Gulu, Masindi and Jinja, and the Kingdom of Buganda, with its hereditary ruler the Kabaka in his palace on Mengo hill, on the outskirts of Kampala, the commercial capital of the country. Buganda had a special status by virtue of a formal Agreement with HMG; the equivalent of the Provincial Commissioner there, keeping an eye on the Kabaka, was known as the Resident, Buganda. The administrative capital, with the government Secretariat and many of the departmental headquarters, was in Entebbe, 21 miles from Kampala, on a beautiful verdant peninsula on the shores of Lake Victoria, where most of the most senior government officials had their houses. His Excellency the Governor lived there too, in Government House, a spacious mansion in a

37

rather Spanish style of architecture, in its own extensive grounds and gardens.

The provinces and Buganda itself were divided into districts, each with its own headquarters, where a District Commissioner (in Buganda a Government Agent) held sway — great men in their own areas. In the Western Province three districts also had their own hereditary rulers: Ankole, Bunyoro and Toro. The peoples in Buganda, Western Province and the adjacent parts of the Eastern all belonged to the Bantu group of Africans: their languages, customs and traditions were all closely related to each other. The peoples in the Northern Province and those in the North of the Eastern were mainly Nilotics. Apart from our first two years in Mbale we spent all our time in Uganda amongst the Bantu; we got to know something of their languages and customs, and I hardly visited the North at all. However I think it is fair to say that the Nilotic Africans and the Bantu resembled each other physically as little as the Swedes and the Italians, and their languages and customs were totally different. Our traditional colonial system, known as 'indirect rule' was to delegate progressively more powers of local government to the existing tribal authorities. The system worked well up to independence: it enabled us, with very limited resources of manpower, to establish conditions of stability in which the economy, education, public health and public order could and did develop and flourish. It did, however, foster local tribal rather than national selfconsciousness and loyalty, and our Western systems of government are in any case alien to African traditions, so that when we left on independence there remained no neutral referee to mediate when intertribal suspicions or conflicts arose: *Hinc illae lacrimae!*

There was also a very considerable Asian community. These were largely the descendants of men who originally come out to East Africa to work on the construction of the railway, but by our time they formed a prosperous group of shopkeepers, artisans, clerical workers, and a few doctors, and they included some very wealthy entrepreneurs, many indeed pillars of the new society, but a few of perhaps rather dubious honesty.

Hindus, Sikhs, Goans, Muslims (including an industrious

Mbale

community of followers of the Agha Khan) all lived together amicably, and maintained an activity in trade and minor industry which contributed greatly to the country's economy, depending as it did largely on the export of African peasant grown cotton and coffee.

The Europeans (Bazungu) were mainly British government servants, but there were also some tea planters and tin miners in the West, — and the occasional stray settler, by now getting old, who had come on from Kenya in the 20s. There were a considerable number of missionaries, both Catholic and Protestant: among the Catholics, Dutch Mill Hill Fathers in the East; French Canadian White Fathers in the West, and Italian Verona Fathers in the North. The Protestants were mostly anglican CMS, but there were also a few Seventh Day Adventists. All in all I don't think the Europeans then numbered more than about 3,000.

Such, briefly, was the new world in which I found myself.

Mbale was the headquarters of two Districts: Bugisu comprised the mountainous country on the Eastern and Northern slopes of Mount Elgon, a huge extinct volcano, over 14,000ft high and 40 miles in circumference, on the Kenya border; the other, Bukedi, the plains leading westwards towards the Nile. The town, which was about the size of Hay-on-Wye, consisted largely of corrugated iron Asian dukas (shops); there was also a government hospital and a CMS church. Behind the town to the east rose a wooded rocky outcrop of Mt. Elgon, Mt. Nkokonjeru; the District Offices, the houses and bungalows of the European officers, the golf course, the club and the swimming pool were all between the town and the slopes of Nkokonjeru. A large forestry plantation was on the south side of the golf course. At an altitude of about 3,000ft on the equator the climate was quite pleasant: hot but not oppressively so. Mosquitoes flourished and we slept under nets, but for us malaria was not a hazard, provided we obediently took our prophylactics, first mepacrine which made you slightly yellow, and later paludrine. I remember the nursing sister saying one day, almost regretfully, "Funny we haven't had a case of blackwater fever for 18 months now".

At first I found living in tropical suburbia rather strange, and it was difficult to occupy the mornings. John, the junior ADC (Assistant District Commissioner) left our bungalow at 0730 to start the station labour force on the vital anti-malarial task of mowing the golf course. Eastern Province was considered hotter than elsewhere, so officials worked what were known as 'Eastern Province hours', which meant that the offices opened early, and closed, without a break, at 1.30pm, when the DC and his staff all went to the local bar for about two hours. It was of course important to keep in touch with what was going on in the Asian community. That meant that I was lucky if we ate before 3.30. Then at 4.0 we went to the club, and played tennis, or golf, or swam till 6.0 when it got dark, and the serious drinking started, accompanied by stories, singing and playing lying dice, until about 10pm, when we went home to supper and bed. On festive occasions there would be parties which lasted until after midnight. As I said before, there were not many wives around in 1946, and it was very much a male-dominated society.

Our household consisted of Yusuf our cook, George William Bosa the head boy so called, but really a Major Domo, Sunguru the 'kitchen toto' or scullion, and a gardener whose name I have forgotten. William had been head boy to a Provincial Commisioner, no less, who was on leave when John arrived, and who had paid him 40s a month and find your own food (by comparison John himself was then on £400 a year, on which we were never in debt). John offered him 45s, so he came and stayed with us. He knew 24 different ways of folding napkins, and thought us very ignoble. When later we were going off to climb Mt. Elgon, and told him we weren't going to take a table with us, he said, "Kama maskini!" — "Like beggars!", and took no further interest in the expedition. I tried to grow various flowers and vegetables. Peas never worked properly: it was too hot and they became hard and bullet-like too fast, but French beans were a success. In fact, certainly in our time, they were a common crop for Africans too, where the conditions suited.

I used to go 'on safari' with John. Each District was subdivided into Sazas, with a council run by the Saza Chief; in turn the Sazas were subdivided into Gombololas, each with its council and Gombolola Chief. Think of County and District Councils here. The Sazas and Gombololas had their own courts, and were responsible for raising local poll taxes. The DC and his ADCs would go round from time to time visiting the Sazas and Gombololas to hear complaints, take appeals from the court judgements, audit the revenue collections, adjudicate applications for exemption from tax, and exhort the people to adopt sound practices in agriculture, public health etc etc. While John spent the mornings doing all this I would explore the bush. Paths led everywhere; in fact if you found the right path in Africa you could walk from coast to coast as the early explorers did, so I never bothered about getting lost. In the late afternoon after work John joined me, and we explored together. We stayed in government rest houses or shelters built in traditional African style. A choo (Swahili), kiyigo (Luganda), latrine (English) was outside. This was a deep hole in the ground covered by a small round hut. Our beds, cooking things etc. were taken out from Mbale in a truck, together with Yusuf to cook and William to keep us all in order. After our evening meal, usually chicken washed down with whisky, we would play piquet by the light of a pressure lamp, swotting mosqitoes, until we had a bath in a canvas bath, got into our camp beds, and tucked in the mosquito nets for the night. After a few weeks of this I found myself pregnant. However apart from some nausea I felt quite well, and early in April, taking advantage of the long Easter weekend, we went up Elgon in a leisurely way with a large convoy of porters carrying stores and a huge tent, and dragging up a sheep behind them. We first camped in bamboo forest at 9,000ft, and on the second day among giant heathers and lobelias — and now in pouring rain — at 11,000ft. There the unhappy sheep was killed and eaten. The next day we went on to the top with a guide. The walking, over a wet moorland, was easy and the altitude no problem, but it was still pouring and in the dense mist we had no views at all. But never mind, we had made it. We then went straight down to the bamboos. The final descent was steep and slippery, and there was a certain dispute among the porters as to who was going to carry the by now soaking wet and even heavier tent. Eventually it was the two weakest who were made to take it. Years later in Nepal John took a photograph of our two oldest porters on trek there, also carrying the heaviest loads.

David was born in the Nakasero Hospital in Kampala on September 11th 1947. In those days European wives were not allowed to give birth in District hospitals due to lack of proper emergency facilities. So we had to spend two weeks before the estimated date of birth in Kampala awaiting events. This was all right later when we had kind friends available to put us up, but we knew no one then, and I was not looking forward to two weeks advance board and lodging in the hospital. John had driven me up, and taken the opportunity to have his wisdom teeth out; that night he was bloody-mouthed and a misery, not thinking of me or impending childbirth at all. However David spared me all the waiting, and took John's mind off his own troubles, by arriving two weeks early, thus allowing John the pleasure of pacing the verandah outside the labour ward, chain smoking, during the process. He then drove back to Mbale, leaving me for another two weeks in hospital. It is odd the way medical theory changes: our mothers had to spend four tedious weeks in bed after giving birth; I had to spend a week in bed after David was born, and then another week in hospital. But then, 16 years later, when Richard was born and I wouldn't have minded a few days rest, I was bundled off in 48 hours. At the time each theory was considered the ultimate in good medical care. I wonder what the next change will be.

After the two weeks David and I went back to Mbale by train. The journey took all day. We stopped at Jinja where kind Pat Few came to the station to see us and give us encouragement, and then proceeded north and east past many small stations. At each stop David woke and yelled. Nothing would stop him except if I fed him, and on each occasion a small excited crowd collected to watch the unfamiliar sight of a Mukazi Muzungu (European Woman) suckling a child. At the Mbale border John met us in the car and took us home. Here I first sampled the full joys of motherhood, helped only by 'Mothercraft in the Tropics' by Kenny Macpherson, sent me by Liz Greaves, and by our new Ayah or nanny, Jeneti Nangobi who then came to us, aged about 19, and was still with us when we left Uganda sixteen years later. By that time we had got to know each other well, but at this stage we each had a lot to learn. However the weeks passed satisfactorily, and by the time we left Mbale in November/Decenber, David was sleeping through the night, which, as any mother knows, and fathers too I expect, is what really matters.

From Mbale we went to Mbarara, the District HQ of Ankole in the Western Province. Ankole is an open hilly country, mainly of grassland, bordering on Ruanda. It was a Bantu district, and its native ruler was the Omugabe, whose father had weighed over 20 stone, and needed a special hoist to get him in and out of his official car. Ankole is also remarkable for its fine immensely long-horned cattle, which roamed the grasslands followed by tall Bahima herdsmen. I always wanted to import some to England. Station life in Mbarara was much the same as in Mbale: tennis, golf, supper parties and club parties. However there were by now many more wives, and women officers too, and the office hours were more normal, so a more regular way of life was practised. But in order to liven things up, from time to time miners and prospectors came in from out of the bush, bringing a different atmosphere with them. We paid a visit once to one of these, Jack Collins, who had some gold workings up in the hills towards the Toro border. John was going on safari the following day, so we arranged for David and Jeneti to accompany the baggage truck, while we left the day before for our visit. We lost our way in the forest, and arrived at 4pm — just the right time for a large lunch with a lot of gin. There was then just time before dark to walk round the extensive garden. Then the serious business began. We sat and talked and drank whisky till midnight, when another large meal arrived, with wine. We then went on drinking — Bols gin, I think — until 0400 when we went to bed. At 0730 Jack came into our hut, fresh as a daisy, with a pint bottle of cold local beer for John. Owing to the weakness of my sex I was spared this, Deo Gratias, but he stood there while John drank it up. Then came a large breakfast with many fried eggs, followed by an about 1½ mile walk through the forest to the place in a stony river bed where a gang of Africans with sieves were panning for gold, and occasionally finding some. Jack gave me a small nugget, very small, which I kept for several years, but it later got stolen. We then walked back through the forest in single file, Jack in front pointing out birds and monkeys and leopard tracks, then me, then John, who took the opportunity to slip into the bush and be sick. Luckily Jack didn't notice, or else John's reputation would have been gone for ever. A large lunch with more gin brought our visit to an end, and we left Jack alone in the bush with his monkeys and birds, his Africans and gold, and proceeded to our camp, where we found Jeneti and David and all in good order.

While we were in Mbarara John got tick typhus. This can now be cured, but at that time there was nothing for it but to take a lot of Veganin to reduce the high fever and wait for it to work itself out, hoping that your heart didn't give up first. John first felt the symptoms after a Saturday party. Quite

44

pardonably, I think, I assumed it was a hangover, and assured him that a good game of tennis would get rid of it. But it didn't, and when next morning he had a temperature of 104° I got the District Medical Officer to come, Jock Black. an ex ships doctor. The symptoms baffled him, so next day his African assistant came with a red drench in a beer bottle. This didn't do any good either, so the next day, rather to my relief, John was put in the back of the nursing sister's little car, with his temperature now 105°, and driven by her down to Kampala, 150 miles over rough roads, with more Veganin whenever the fever recurred. There the very able consultant diagnosed it instantly, and on the following day demonstrated the symptoms of the disease to his African medical students over John's recumbent body. So John remained in bed for a fortnight until the fever was exhausted, by which time he weighed 9 stone.

Shortly after this John heard that he was to go back to England for six months, to go on the 2nd Devonshire Course (so called after a former Colonial Secretary). At that time it was still assumed that the Empire would continue for a long time yet, and prospective colonial service officers were given preliminary training in what to expect (and what was expected of them). The 1st Devonshire Course was for beginners; the 2nd for officers who already had had some experience, so John was chosen for that, and was to take his entitlement of leave at the same time.

11. August 1948 — April 1949:
Return to England and Return Again

We left Uganda by train for Nairobi at the end of July. The journey was uneventful except for David who fell on the floor when the train stopped suddenly outside Eldoret. However, after some howling he went to sleep again. From

Nairobi we flew to Aden in a Dakota, with seats this time. Nairobi in August is pleasantly cool; we came down to Aden through clouds, and when the doors opened it was like going into a steam bath. There was no air conditioning in the Government House guest house where we slept, and the humidity was trying. John and I had some of our best quarrels, but managed to appear good humoured in public and in the presence of his parents. I remember pleasant picnics at the swimming club at Gold Mohur, where steel nets protected the beach from the sharks, an early morning ascent of Shum Shum with John's father, the Governor — and a very amusing party.

An Argentine training cruiser with an admiral on board was paying a courtesy visit to Aden, and there was to be a grand official dinner for their senior officers. The ADC at the time was one Major Ken Nichol. John's mother was an almost perfect mother-in-law, which must sometimes have tried her sorely as she had high standards, and these made her intolerant of the usual casual young ADCs, the turnover of whom at GH was fast. However she met her match in Ken Nichol, Uncle as we called him, who was older than she was, so he virtually did as he pleased. Word had come that the Argentinians spoke no English, so John's father said that they must be made to speak with the tongues of angels. Uncle accordingly prepared preliminary cocktails, in identical cocktail shakers, of three strengths: one for the Argentinians, one for the male British and one for the ladies. Awful sexual discrimination of course, but common in those unenlightened times. Just before the guests were due to arrive an unexpected storm caused the cruiser to shift her moorings, and all her officers had to remain on board. It was too late to cancel the party, but Uncle had to go and change the place settings, leaving John, as his temporary assistant, in charge of the drinks which all looked identical. Chaos resulted. The guests were all now senior colonial officials and their wives. Those who had started with the weak drinks promptly had more; whoever had an Argentinian one was well away in no time, and the only sober person was the wife of the Director of Medical Services, a teetotaller, who stuck to lemonade. Champagne was on offer for the dinner; medals and decorations were the rig of the day, and the Attorney General's Brilliant Star of Zanzibar was hanging over the back of his neck before the main course. The noise was terrific, but not loud enough to drown Uncle's voice shouting to the staff: "Bring on more champagne!" Next morning the Governor went off to his office feeling quite poorly; his wife said it served him right.

John's course was to start early in September, so he left on the Blue Funnel MV *Priam* in mid August, and I stayed on a little while longer, going on by the *Astyanax* on which my brother Stopford (Tiny) was then a midshipman. David was not yet walking, but he was an active crawler, so John's mother made him a set of reins. I tied these to the ship's rail, and so David was able to crawl happily about, picking up and eating cigarette ends out of the scuppers while Stopford and I and others enjoyed ourselves leaning on the rails and drinking gin. None of us seemed to come to any harm, including David.

John's course, of two academic terms, started with a couple of weeks in Cambridge, and was then based in the SOAS (School of Oriental and African Studies) in London. He had a bed sitter with bath off the Cromwell Road, where I paid him occasional visits. Once we attempted to clean some of the paint work in his room: a mistake, as this merely accentuated the remaining deep layers of grime. Breakfasts and evening meals were also provided; John said he had seldom had worse.

David and I went down to Pencraig. Much of the furniture from 52 had been put into store during the war and destroyed in an air raid, and in any case no one then had any money, and a return to 52 was impractical, so my father gave back the lease to the City Council, who pulled the house down and built flats in its place. My parents moved to Riversdale Road, where they lived until my father retired in 1952. However Pencraig was kept for holidays and week ends, and David and I spent the next few months there. Mistrusting my maternal skills my mother engaged a professional Norland nanny, Nurse Peterson, a great snob: all her previous employers had had titles except us. She flung up her hands in horror at my methods (no more cigarette ends!), and I must

47

say that David flourished under her treatment and plumped out considerably. She potty trained him by the simple expedient of putting him, on the pot, in the corner of his playpen, and tying him to the bars. It worked. We were therefore able to leave David in her capable care, and go to Switzerland during the winter vacation. We stayed in the Kulm Hotel in Lenzerheide where John had spent a family holiday in the 30s. The tourist skiers had hardly begun to take over yet, and Lenzerheide as I remember it was small and rural, bacon hung in the hotel garage, and there was only one ski-lift. John knew, vaguely, how to ski. I spent most of my time falling down. We made two quite long day trips, and I remember on one of them, as it was getting dark and already freezing, picking myself up from the hard bumpy snow, and hearing from far down the slope a familiar voice shouting, "For God's sake, come ON". So I set off again until the next fall.

At the end of March 1949 John's course came to an end, and we returned to Uganda, again via Aden where his father was still the Governor. Unfortunately I cannot remember the name of the ship (it must have been a 12 passenger berth vessel going to the Far East), which is a pity as the voyage is associated with one great character, Father Gover. However, whatever the ship, David and I set off on her from Birkenhead, and at Rotterdam John joined us, having come straight over from London. I remember the Blue Funnel agent kindly taking us for a drive through Holland during the afternoon: a very dull country, I thought.

Apart from Father Gover I only remember two of our fellow passengers, a missionary and his wife going to Japan, but Father Gover was unforgettable. He was a naval padre on his way to Hong Kong. His last time in the tropics had been in the West Indies, and since then his shape had enlarged considerably. Clothes in 1949 were still hard to come by, and in order to make his lightweight trousers fit a large gusset had been put in at the back, unfortunately in a darker colour from the rest of the trousers. This was particularly noticeable when he knelt down to pray: he took a service every Sunday — and a good one too. Every day at lunch-time he would have four large ship's pink gins, but five on Sundays because "preaching was thirsty work". In the afternoons as we walked round the deck with David we would see him through the saloon windows asleep with his hands clasped over his ample stomach. In the evenings he would drink "Tigers' Kisses", that is to say a double rum, a double brandy and a port all together in a tumbler! I never saw him in any way the worse for all this.

On our arrival at Port Said the usual bum-boats came alongside selling tourist wares, which were hoisted up to the deck for inspection in baskets, which in turn took down the money if the sale was on. While we were leaning over the rail watching all this the missionary looked forward towards the crews quarters and said, "Fancy, they're selling books". Pornography was not as freely available in the UK as it is now. "Books!" said Father Gover, "I'll soon put a stop to that!", and off he went, and soon we saw his portly figure on the foredeck gesticulating angrily, while the crew sheepishly lowered the offending literature back to the rather bewildered hawkers in the boats below.

After a short stay in Aden we went over to Nairobi, this time by Aden Airways, stopping at Hargeisa in what was then British Somaliland, and at Mogadishu in Italian Somaliland. David ran away during the stop at Hargeisa airport — only a hut on a sandy landing strip — and had to be brought back from the desert. We had to make an unscheduled night stop for engine trouble at Mogadishu, in a hotel called 'Il Croce del Sud', very basic, but with a beautiful courtyard garden (We've just heard that it still exists to-day, accommodating journalists and relief workers covering the current famine and chaos; I don't envy them!). I remember that the shower in the 'bathroom' was operated by a string, which on being pulled released a few drops of tepid water: rather frustrating. There were also a lot of mosquitoes, but the nets were good, and David slept peacefully in his cot beside us. We hadn't realised that our bill was going to be paid by the airline, so restricted ourselves to an omelette and some locally made whisky, and were annoyed when we discovered next morning that we could have had whatever we had wanted. I do not remember the journey onwards from Nairobi, but in due course we found ourselves back in Uganda, this time in Entebbe for John to do a tour in government headquarters, the Secretariat.

12. April 1949 — July 1952: Entebbe

As I said before, the Entebbe that I remember was on a peninsula on the shores of Lake Victoria about 21 miles from Kampala. It consisted of a golf course, a settlement of bungalows graded according to the status of their occupants, a handsome Government House built on a hill, and an only slightly less handsome Chief Secretary's house on a cliff overlooking the lake, a bank, a small hospital, a police station, a cinema, most of the central government offices, the Lake Victoria Hotel, the European Primary School and Kindergarten, a Catholic mission with a large church, a small Protestant church, the Entebbe Club (very important), and the Swimming Club — for Bazungu (whites) only of course. On the hill above Government House was the Yelllow Fever Research Institute. The police lines and the African hospital were at the Kampala end of town, with a forestry plantation on the outskirts. Beside the lake there were the fine botanic gardens, and a small harbour and pier where the Lake Victoria steamers used to call, with the Geological Survey Department's offices behind. On the other side of the town was a small international airport, and a beach, on which our children could play and paddle in the lake, and from which the local fishermen went off in their big canoes to catch ngege, the delicious lake carp. Beyond again, on Old Entebbe hill, was the Veterinary Research station.

The climate was pleasant once you got used to it and the abundant mosquitoes had got used to your taste. The dry season lasted from October to March, and the rains

Entebbe – Our first house

followed, but as with most climates there were often surprises. A particular feature of the place were the lake flies. These great swarms of tiny flies, smaller than midges but thankfully not biting, would rise in certain conditions from far out in the lake; you could watch them in grey clouds approaching on the wind, and soon your house would be swamped in them — you too if you got in their way. They had a persistent rather fishy odour, and the Africans would sweep them in piles off the floor and make porridgy cakes out of them, which were said to be tasty, but I never tried any.

It was here that we were to spend the next three and a half years. Apart from the manager of the NBI (National Bank of India) and his family all the Europeans were government officials — unlike the situation in Kampala where there was a considerable commercial community. When we arrived the Governor was Sir John Hathorn Hall, who had preceded John's father as Governor of Aden. His predecessor in

Entebbe, Sir Charles Dundas, had had an American wife about whom there were many stories, including one to the effect that she had started an address to a meeting of prominent local European ladies, "Ladies of Entebbe! Women of Kampala!" Whether true or not the story indicates a certain social distinction between the two communities.

John was posted to the Secretariat G1 section. His work covered security, home affairs, refugees — including efforts to resettle the remnants of a large camp of Polish wartime refugees who had ultimately fetched up in Uganda, via Siberia and the Persian Gulf, after being interned by the Russians, and undesirables from all over the middle east interned as security risks by our own people at the crisis of the war there. He was also concerned with relations with the Colonial Office and the other East African territories, and questions of nationality. We arrived just at the time of riots in Buganda, a foreshadowing of the future, as the Baganda were trying to assert their own separate independence. They were to do this again several times subsequently, until they were finally crushed by Obote after Uganda itself became independent years later. Most of the rioting took place by day in and around Katwe, a seedy African suburb of Kampala on the road from Entebbe. While awaiting the arrival of our new grey Standard Vanguard from England John had borrowed an old clapped out car from a colleague. Late every night while the riots lasted he had to collect the official communiqué on the day's events from the Government Printer in Entebbe, and deliver it to Kampala for publication first thing on the following day, dodging the litter of the previous day's rioting as he went through Katwe. Fortunately the old car managed not to break down or get a puncture as he did so.

The riots did not last long, and we settled down to what was a pleasant way of life. David kept me busy, and I soon found myself pregnant with Lawrence. Normal office hours were observed, and in the afternoons after work John would play golf, or we would walk along the beach, over the bush beyond Old Entebbe, or around the Botanic Gardens. Socially we made many friends, some of whom we have kept

Lawrence about
to be pushed
down by David...

in touch with ever since, such as Henry and Hazel Morris, Pat and Selwyn Few (Selwyn now alas gone), Paul and Gill Gore, Brian and Nancy Kirwan, Charles and Diana Fulford-Williams, and Bill and Diana Rae of the Bank. La crême de la crême of Entebbe social life was the 'Hard Core'. This consisted of about eight people, centering around Dermot Sheridan a witty, brilliant Crown Counsel crippled by childhood polio, but gallant and charming — and a really hard drinker. Much later, as I think Chief Justice after independence, he was murdered between Kampala and Entebbe. We never belonged to the Hard Core, but were invited occasionally to their parties; the mornings after were a serious ordeal. Of course if you showed any sign during the party of not being able to "hold your liquor" you would never get invited to another.

My mother came to stay at the end of 1949. She came by flying boat to Port Bell where we met her. Unlike myself she loved flying, and really enjoyed the several trips out she made, because she loved Africa as much as I did. Lawrence was born early on New Year's Day 1950. He must have inconvenienced the Scottish doctor, who had to interrupt his Hogmanay party to deliver him. He was a wonderful baby: just eating, sleeping and smiling. David took no notice of him until he started to walk, when he took much pleasure in darting up behind him and pushing him down. Jeneti soon put a stop to that. Both little boys thrived, and even whooping cough in 1951 was no serious trouble. John's

parents also visited us in 1951 on their way home to retire.
Our household continued with various changes, the most traumatic being the departure of George William Bosa. Jeneti was the daughter of an important Musoga chief. He had 36 wives and about 200 children. Jeneti was the daughter of one of his senior wives, and as such, expected to play her part in the care and upbringing of junior members of the family. At this time, I think in 1951, she had Mary, aged seven, living with her. One evening I was reading Benjamin Bunny to the two little boys, — John was of course at the club after golf — when there was a great shouting and outcry in the kitchen, and Jeneti burst in, dragging Mary by the hand, and turned her upside down for me to look at. I gathered that William had "haribu"-ed (destroyed) Mary. The children stared. By now I was getting used to dealing with domestic rows and problems, so I said that I was no doctor, and that she'd better take Mary to the hospital. Things then calmed down, and next day Mary was taken to the hospital, where she was found to have what was then known as "a dose of clap". Police then came and took William away to the hospital where, surprisingly, he too was found to be similarly infected. However, as he indignantly denied the accusation, and it was only Mary's word and circumstantial evidence against him, there was no case to be taken in the Protectorate Courts. So Jeneti took him to the native court which was not bound by strict Anglo-Saxon laws of evidence, but where justice was done, and he was fined 250/-, the price of his new bicycle. His confidence then collapsed, and he accepted dismissal without protest. The reason for the assault on Mary had been the commonly held belief among Africans that VD can be cured by lying with a virgin. In this case there was a happy ending, as both William and Mary were in fact cured by antibiotics. It is, however indicative of the problem of finding common ground among people of different cultures that when, after it was all over, as Jeneti and I were shaking our heads, she said to me, as I was thinking of the poor little girl, "Yes, I can't understand it. William and I have been with you for five years now, and we have never quarrelled. He knew I was Mary's guardian. If he wanted her, why didn't he ask me first?" Luckily on this

occasion we came to the same conclusion, albeit by different paths: William had to go.

In December 1951 my third child, a girl, was born. Alas, she was dead on arrival — why no one was ever sure, as there had been no problems beforehand. It was a great shock to me: disasters until then had been something that happened to other people. Also one of the added trials of such a misfortune is that not only is the little life lost, but you yourself have all your hormone balance upset for six weeks afterwards; there is not only sadness and disappointment but also physical discomfort. The experience revealed more differences between the British and the Africans, to the credit, I think, of the latter. When I got back to Entebbe our close friends were all most kind, but those who knew me less well were clearly embarrassed, and would cross the road to avoid me. Not so the Africans: Jeneti's friends, the vegetable seller, the ayahs (nannies) of our childrens' friends, all came to call, took me by the hands and made appropriate remarks: "Ee nyabo, kitalo, kitalo nnyo", ("Oh madam, how awful, how very awful!"). This made me feel better. I think that they, being less cossetted against death than we are, know better how to treat the afflicted.

It was about this time, early 1952, that Andrew Cohen became Governor, and John was asked to postpone the home leave to which we were by then entitled to be his Private Secretary for six months. Cohen was young for a Governor, intellectually brilliant, but with no social graces, and a ruthless taskmaster. John would often return home late in the evening, drained and speechless, until revived by a very stiff whisky while having a hot bath before supper. But often, just when the situation seemed to be becoming intolerable, Cohen would suddenly show a surprising and touching kindness, as when, on John's birthday (which we had no reason to expect that Cohen would have known), he summoned him away from home at almost no notice to accompany him on tour, but then, in the evening in the bush, presented him with rather a nice book to make amends.

It was also at this time that I had my first, and last I hope, really bad attack of malaria. John was away with Cohen in Nairobi when I first began to have 'flu like symptoms. By midnight all the blankets were on the bed, and I was shuddering with cold; shortly afterwards I sweated so much that the bed was soaked to the mattress; then I felt slightly better. After about three hours the process started again. It served me right, as I had been slack about taking my anti-malarial pills. Next morning the doctor came and diagnosed malignant subtertian, which sounded pretty impressive and cheered me up. Injections of quinine and mepacrine got rid of it, but I never missed taking my prophylactics again. One bonus was that I lost a great deal of weight without any moral effort.

Towards the end of that February King George VI died. Princess Elizabeth and the Duke of Edinburgh were on a tour of Kenya when this happened, staying in the Tree Tops hotel Of course she had to return to England at once, and was flown in a light plane to Entebbe, where RAF aircraft were sent to fetch her home that same evening. There was a mix up in the arrangements, and the royal party were delayed for some hours in Entebbe, where the Cohens, with John in attendance, of course had to receive them. As indicated, small talk to a newly bereaved Queen would not have been Cohen's strongest point, and after a couple of hours in the airport lounge, it now being dark and raining heavily, the young Queen decided to board her waiting aircraft, and John had the privilege of folding Lady (Helen) Cohen's voluminous mackintosh around his sovereign's smaller shoulders on the day of her accession, feeling like a modern Sir Walter Raleigh.

The Cohens went on several safaris and John went with them. I joined him for one in the Western Province which ended in Kigezi, where there was a good hotel I took the car and the children and met the Governor's party at Kabale after a night's stay with friends in Masaka, where there was a jolly lunchtime drinks party with the children wandering around; Lawrence, then aged two, swallowed up all the heel taps. He was very fractious after his evening nap. Kabale was a beautiful place in hilly country on the Congo border, with lakes and volcanoes. We spent several holidays there, including one with John's parents when they were with us in 1951. On this occasion I remember the chore of having to sew black armbands (for the late King) onto both John's and Cohen's official white uniforms before a formal parade. It was very difficult to get the wretched things straight.

During most of John's time as Private Secretary there was official court mourning, so there was no large scale entertaining at Government House. However when court mourning ended the Cohens decided to celebrate in style, with a great dance and a live African band. No such thing had ever been seen in GH before. I remember being much taken with the band's rendering of '*J'attendrai*'. Cohen mixed the punch himself, and omitted to include any dilutant, but only one young KAR subaltern had to be asked to leave the floor. John had an unexpected call to duty when he was told that the men's toilet was overflowing. The Deputy Director of Public Works (a former sewage engineer) came to the rescue in his white tie and tails, and plunged his arm down the loo, but to no avail. He did not seem too popular as a dance partner afterwards, but the party ended fortunately before the house was flooded.

Our first tour in Entebbe ended early in July 1952. We flew back to England, taking 24 hours, with stops at Khartoum, Tripoli and Rome. We were ahead of time, and in brilliant sunshine the pilot flew us all round the summit of Mont Blanc on our way to Heathrow, where we took delivery of another new Standard Vanguard, this time a black one, and set off for Scotland.

13. July 1952 — December 1952: Leave and return to Uganda

Before the time of self-catering holiday cottages it was the custom in the Scottish Highlands for the owners of good farm houses or crofts to let them in the summer to people from Glasgow and Edinburgh, moving themselves to camp in the farm outbuildings — just the opposite to what happens now in fact. However the farmer's wife kept the use of her own kitchen, and provided meals for the tenants. It was to one such farm, Achosnich, on the moor above and to the west of Grantown-on-Spey that we went in the new Vanguard to stay until early October. On the way there we spent a few days in Edinburgh to see John's grandmother, Amy Macgregor, widow of the Very Revd Principal WM Macgregor, the ex Moderator of the United Free Church of Scotland, the mother of Aunt Bo of Nagasaki fame. The old lady was by now rising 95 and becoming a little confused, but still quite active. We tried hard to impress on David, by now nearly five, how special it was to meet one's great-grandmother, but in vain: all he can remember of the visit is feeding the swans in the Braids Park. There was no room for us all with Granny in Braid Avenue, so we stayed in a nearby guest house. While there David and Lawrence behaved very well, and it wasn't until later that we learned that they had been busy with wax crayons re-decorating the walls of their bedroom. I think it cost us £35, quite a lot of money then, to replace the wallpaper.

Achosnich was comfortable, and the owners were very friendly, The surrounding country was beautiful and wild, and it was a pity that during the three months we were there it rained for some, though not all, of every day except three, and there was snow on the hills in August. However once I had bought some woollen underwear I got used to it and we all enjoyed ourselves. John would go and play golf in the mornings, while the children and I walked in the pine woods around the course; we went for picnics, and visited all the sites of the Macgregor legend. John's parents came and stayed in Grantown for two weeks, and also his brother Tony, who was by then a prep school master, and came with his friends the De Torrs — Ken and wife and daughter. Ken, an ex RSM, was sports master at St Bede's School in Eastbourne, and a very kindly and congenial character. It was impossible with the small children to do any of the long walks we should otherwise have enjoyed, but looking after David and Lawrence absorbed most of our time and energies, especially as they both woke with the dawn, which in

Scotland at that time of year comes about 0330.

One afternoon we were all invited to tea by Cousin Anne (see Chapter 5). She now lived in some style, surrounded by delicate *objets d'art* in a house in Nethybridge, her mother, Aunt Eliza having now died, and she had prepared a lavish tea with all sorts of delicacies and cream cakes for the little boys, who, however, only wanted bread and butter and to have a romp. It was a relief to be able to turn them out to play on the lawn — at least until Lawrence came running in again without his trousers, having used the lawn for a minor purpose, as he had been accustomed to do in the freedom of Africa. I don't think Cousin Anne had seen anything of the like in her life before, but she was very gracious about it.

On our return south we stopped again, briefly, in Edinburgh. Here there was sadness. The old lady had had a fall and broken a hip; pneumonia followed, and left alone she could have ended her long and well-lived life in dignity and not too painfully, but it was not to be. Antibiotics were prescribed, and the poor old thing, by now just skin and bone, was kept alive for another two months with daily, excruciatingly painful injections. We saw her briefly; she could hardly recognise even John, and it is a sad last memory for me — and was still more so for John, whom she brought up as a second mother for some years as a delicate small boy sent home to avoid the Middle Eastern climate. I am not going into the arguments for or against euthanasia, but I am sure there is a time to let people go.

During the month remaining of our time in England we made several family visits, including one to LPJ, by now 91, quite fit and living at Far Outlook on Shotover Hill outside Oxford, and looked after by a housekeeper, Miss George. My grandmother had died in 1945. Again we tried to impress on David the unique interest of a great-grandfather, but again in vain, but there is a photograph of them together to prove it. John's father on retiring from the Colonial Service had decided to go into the church, and was by now serving his curacy at Maidstone. We went to hear his very first sermon, to a packed evensong in Maidstone parish church (someone else must have looked after David and Lawrence). He had a fine preaching voice, and was very handsome with

59

Olive　L.P.J.　John
　David　Lawrence
at Far Outlook – October 1952

his silver hair, and he gave a moving sermon on the sufferings and injustices of Palestinian refugees in consequence of the Balfour Declaration and all that flowed from it. John and I agreed with every word, but wondered how many others in the congregation knew what he was talking about. John heard two old ladies saying as they came out of the church, "Didn't follow all he were saying — but weren't he luvly!"

We went to Pencraig for the last time. My father was retiring that year, aged 70, and although he would have been content to live in Pencraig, my mother, who was 18 years younger and knew she would have some time on her own, wanted to find somewhere more English to live. It was sad to say 'Good Bye' to Pencraig, but I am sure that my mother was right. After a great deal of searching they decided on Herefordshire, not far from Aunt Molly, and bought our present house, Farmore, from a Dr. Wells, who had himself bought it in 1938 from the Church Commissioners, with five acres, for £700. It had previously been the rectory for the little Parish of Dewsall with Callow. Mother and I went down to look at the house after the Wellses had moved out. We stayed at the Green Dragon in Hereford, and came out on a damp November morning and walked round the empty house. I remember thinking that there was going to be plenty to keep her occupied.

In November we left Liverpool by Blue Funnel for the last time, on MV *Agapenor*. I remember nothing about the voyage except that in the Red Sea while bathing Lawrence a sudden lurch flung me into the bath on top of him, and I pushed him under. However he came up spluttering, and I don't think he holds it against me. We stayed a while in Aden again, this time with Liz and Tom, who were living there and were very kind. I remember jolly picnics at Gold Mohur. From Aden we flew to Nairobi uneventfully, and from there on to Entebbe, where our luck ran out for the moment. John had been posted to Fort Portal in Toro District in the Western Province as ADC (Assistant District Commissioner), and we were going to collect the old Vanguard (while the new black one was coming out by sea), and drive up there in a couple of days. Meanwhile we were going to stay in the Lake Victoria Hotel. We arrived in the early evening, and colleagues, Geoffrey and Ann Greenwood, who lived next door to the hotel, asked us out to supper. After some hesitation we decided to go. David and Lawrence were, after all, experienced travellers, and seemed quite relaxed and happy. So, explaining that we wouldn't be going far or for long, we said "Good night", and left them. When we came back through the hotel doors at about 10.30pm I could hear a sound of distant yelling, and the nearer we got to our rooms the louder it became, and there outside the boys' door was the angry and nasty South African manager, two very nice Canadians, Ron and Peggy Harvie, whom we were to get to know very well in Fort Portal, and had come to be helpful — and Lawrence, who had been sick, and David who in his efforts to help in the dark had broken a water bottle. Broken glass, water, sick and worse were all over the floor, and both boys (not to speak of the manager) were hysterical. By now I was six months pregnant with Sally and anxious to be careful, so I decided it would be best if I stayed out of the fracas, and retreated to our own bedroom, leaving it to John to sort out the mess...

Next day we left Lake Victoria Hotel in disgrace, and fled to stay with Paul and Gill Gore, who were all that good friends should be. They took us that evening to a pantomime given by the KATS (Kampala Amateur Theatrical Society). I don't remember what the pantomime was, but I do remember that it involved firing a revolver fairly often. At each shot Sally inside me gave the most alarming leaps, thereby revealing early signs of her lively temperament.

By now it was nearly Christmas, so on the way to Fort Portal we stopped at Mubende, the last place in Buganda before the Toro border, where our friends Eric and Peggy Lanning were living with their children. Eric was the Government Agent there. We stayed several times with them, and I came to know Mubende hill quite well. This time we stayed in the Rest House, looking out over the plains towards the distant Ruwenzori, and recovered from the traumas of the Lake Victoria Hotel. There was a party for the station children in the Lanning house, which had fireplaces as it could be quite cold at that altitude. The District Police Officer dressed himself up as Father Christmas and pretended to come down the chimney. All the children were called to come up and get their presents from him, but Lawrence, not quite three, was scared and had to be taken out screaming. So after all this excitement it was a relief finally to reach Fort Portal.

14. Fort Portal:
January 1953 — October 1954

Fort Portal when we went there was in size little more than a village, in spite of recently having become the HQ of the Western Province: Masindi had been the previous HQ. It was situated just below the eastern slopes of the Ruwenzori Mountains, and looked over a country of wooded hills and banana plantations. At 5,000ft the climate was not troublesome. The government offices and the officials' bungalows were on a slight hill to the north of the main street, culminating in the Mountains of the Moon Hotel, and with the Provincial Commissioner's new Bungalow overlooking it all. The golf course was to the east, with a forestry plantation on one side of it, and the prison at the far end. In the centre of the government complex was the club, built on what had been the original fort and still surrounded by the remains of a moat. Beyond to the south was the main street of Asian dukas, with the African market, and then, climbing up the hill, were the two large mission stations, Catholic and Protestant of course — there was never one without the other: competition for souls was fierce — and finally the palace of the hereditary ruler, the Omukama, overlooking both. So the Protectorate and the native rulers faced each other, quite amicably, over the trading centre. There was also a large CMS secondary school a short way out of town. Behind it all to the west, bisected by the Equator and usually clouded in mist, rose the great mass of the

Ruwenzori range, 60 miles in length, and rising to perpetual snowy peaks at over 16,000ft. These were the authentic Mountains of the Moon of legend. Apart from our fellow officials and families there were a number of tea and coffee planters who came in to socialise, and a few miners and prospectors and missionary teachers. In the foothills of Ruwenzori 50 miles south of Fort Portal there was quite a large copper mine run by a Canadian company. The African population of the District of Toro was about 300,000.

Our household here consisted of Polito the cook, Silvesta and Kiiza the house servants, Sarapio, an attractive boy who was the kitchen toto or general dogsbody, Gereson the gardener, and of course Jeneti. Apart from Jeneti all of them were local Batoro, and everyone got on well together. Another most important member of the household was Sheba, who had first come to us in Entebbe as a puppy. She was half Ridgeback and half Labrador, and was the best dog we ever had in Africa, reliable, friendly and gentle with those she knew, but she was yet a formidable watch dog, and guarded us most efficiently. Her only fault was a propensity to enormous litters — she ultimately had 96 puppies. I secluded her zealously each time she came on heat, only to have my efforts sabotaged by Polito, who couldn't see why she should not be allowed to have her usual 16 puppies; each time I was sure I had been successful, only to find after a few weeks that I had not, and to be told, proudly, by Polito, "O yes, Memsahib, and it's that dog of Bwana So and So — a very fine dog" There were no facilities for disposing of unwanted puppies, so I had to learn the hard way how to drown them, swiftly and with minimum suffering all round, because it is not very agreeable to be the executioner.

Sally was born in Kampala on Friday, 13th March 1953. I had gone down to Kampala two weeks before she was due, and stayed in the government hostel. Gill and Paul Gore took care of me, and despite the unpropitious day Sally arrived without any trouble at all, and after two weeks we went back again to Fort Porta. With Sally and the two little boys I was kept busy and happy, and there was also the added interest of teaching David, who was now five. There was then no English speaking school in Fort Portal, so while I was on

Silvester

Kiiza

65

leave I had got in touch with the PNEU, and had books and instruction from them. David and I spent three hours every morning on the three Rs, and I well remember the positive thrill when he began to be able to read; once the breakthrough had been made he progressed at a great rate. It was most rewarding.

In the bungalow next to ours lived Ron and Peggy Harvie, whom we had met in the Lake Victoria Hotel, where they had supported us against the disagreeable manager. Ron was the Agricultural Officer, and they had a little boy, Tom, younger than ours, and we became good friends, playing bridge and tennis together. They had a wonderful dog called Gus. He was a cross between a dachshund and a bull terrier, low on the ground, a powerful chest, and with all the ferocity of the bull terrier he dominated the local canine community. But he never fathered anything on Sheba (though he did on almost every other bitch of his acqaintance). Probably he was too low. John and Ron went on several safaris together into the mountains; with the children I did not go on walking safaris, but we all went with John down to Bundibugyo in Bwamba on several occasions. Bwamba was low down on the north western side of the Ruwenzori, looking over the Semliki Flats to the hills and forests of the Belgian Congo beyond. To get there the road wound round and round and down and down the northern flanks of the mountain to Bundibugyo, at less than 3,000ft. We never made the journey without Lawrence being sick. John and I would go for walks in the forest, and once we saw a pygmy: a tiny, naked man, carrying a little spear and a bow and arrows, run across the track before us as swiftly and silently as the little deer he was probably pursuing. Another amusing episode I remember, which put me in my place. I was walking down the road with David and Lawrence, when an African woman came up in the opposite direction with a baby on her back and a little boy of about Lawrence's age running in front. When he saw us he stopped, horrified, and then dashed screaming back to his mother. She and I both laughed, but whenever I think of it I am sure how foolish the 'politically correct' are to ignore that racial consciousness is an innate part of human nature, and cannot be lightly swept aside.

Polito

There was a game park around the shores of Lake Edward, which lay between Uganda and the Congo. Later this was to become the Queen Elizabeth National Park. The nearest rest camp was at Katwe on the shores of the lake, near where the Kazinga Channel joined it to Lake George. Here hippo and elephant abounded, and we went there several times. On one occasion David was happily playing on the verandah of the rest house, whacking a little shrub with a stick, when out of it slid a thin, bright green snake, which disappeared as rapidly as it had emerged. We never identified it, and do not therefore know whether David had had a brush with a deadly green mamba. The story was current at that time in Fort Portal that the prim wife of the District Medical Officer was just about to settle down on the seat of the loo in the same rest house, when a very large black mamba emerged from the deep hole beneath her. Perhaps Katwe mambas are less agressive than others. It was on one of these trips to Katwe that John and I, Jeneti and the children called on Paul Chapman at his shamba (farm) up on the slopes of the mountain. Paul was an old Etonian; in the first world war he had been ADC to General Smuts, and had since made and lost several fortunes ivory smuggling from the Congo. His last expedition failed; he had his ivory confiscated, and was left almost penniless but still resourceful. So he acquired some land, set trip-wires attached to shotguns around it to discourage animal or human marauders, and built himself a copy of an Anglo-Saxon great hall (or so he thought), the main beams of which were of living wood, the idea being that termites would not eat them. A stream ran through the garden, and he made good use of this. It ran first through his maize mill, then through his hall (so he could wash his plates without leaving the table), and then as a flush for his latrine. I hope nobody drank from it downstream. Visitors always had to take some gin with them. John duly took a large bottle. After we had walked round the shamba we went into the great hall for refreshments. In the middle was a long, dark wooden table with an enamel jug of fine roses in the centre. At the top of this table sat John and Paul Chapman with the gin. Below the roses sat Jeneti and I and the children with a pot of tea. I knew better than to protest, but Jeneti, who was used to racial but not to sexual apartheid was quite bewildered, and whispered a lot to me. Luckily the men were too busy with the gin to notice.

During this time the Lannings from Mubende went on leave. They had a cat called Pepsi who had been suffering severe sexual deprivation, as there were no other cats on Mubende hill, so we offered to remedy this, there being plenty of cats in Fort Portal. Pepsi arrived by bus in a box, and within a few days was made happy, and in due course had a large litter of kittens. When the Lannings came back we put Pepsi and all her kittens into the box and sent them back by the bus. I don't know what Eric and Peggy were expecting, but apparently there was quite a surprise when the box was opened; their house was overrun, and thereafter there was no shortage of cats on Mubende hill.

It was in December of 1953, I think, that the Kabaka of Buganda, not liking his political constraints, got across Cohen and HMG, and was exiled to the UK. The Baganda replied by boycotting Asian shops and by minor rioting. News of this all came through to Toro but did not directly affect us. I think it was in 1954, probably in January, that we went to Mubende again. Eric Lanning was a keen amateur archaeologist, and I remember struggling through bush to find camp sites of the early European explorers, and also a visit to a very smelly cave. It was at this time, too, that we had one of our severest gastronomic ordeals. The leading Asian merchant in Mubende had invited the Government Agent and his friends to lunch. We arrived at 1230, and for three hours were treated to beer and gin and a wide variety of delicious samosas and similar snacks, which we all ate enthusiastically. At 3.30, just as we were getting ready to say 'thank you' and go, there arrived enormous dishes of rice and bowls of curry. Somehow or other we managed to eat enough of it, but it was a sad misunderstanding. Another, though slightly different misunderstanding occurred for us later in Bundibugyo, when John, by then the DC, was there on tour with Andrew Stuart, who had come out to Fort Portal on first appointment as his junior ADC. Again the leading Asian duka owner was entertaining us lavishly. Conversation took place in a mixture of broken English and

Swahili, and we seemed to be getting on well. However towards the end of the evening we understood our host to say that his parrot spoke good Swahili. We were impressed, and said we would very much like to see it. This seemed to cause some embarrassment and delay, but after a while a very old lady, our host's mother, reluctantly appeared, and we realised that he must have said 'parent'. We left as soon as we decently could with many expressions of polite gratitude, thoroughly ashamed of our social ineptitude.

The Queen's coronation was in May 1953. There were celebrations throughout Uganda, but I particularly remember the evening party in Fort Portal, with a bonfire and a barbecued deer, which was held outside the club. Many loyal toasts were drunk and songs sung, increasingly less and less relevant to the occasion. Frank Gibson was in fine voice with "Lloyd George knew my father". Afterwards the DC's wife, Mavis Stone, and Peggy Harvie both got tapeworms. I was lucky that time and didn't. Peggy called her's Horace, and I remember Horace being rather obstinate.

About a year later The Queen and Prince Philip came to see the Queen Elizabeth Park at the end of their world tour, when they were both obviously tired. The Park now had a comfortable tourist rest house and its headquarters at Mweya, on a spectacular neck of land between the Kazinga Channel and Lake Edward. The Mau Mau rebellion had started in Kenya, and royal security had to be taken seriously in Toro. During the visit all Kikuyu in the District were rounded up and held in the police cells in Fort Portal. I remember walking past and seeing crowded black faces pressed against the bars. As the senior ADC John was in charge of security, and on the great day we went down to Katwe just ahead of the royal party to go over their route to see that all was well. It was, and the Queen and the Prince were taken on a tour of the Park, and then given a sit-down meal with one or two of the very top local officials (the food all flown out for the occasion by BOAC — salmon from Scotland, duck from Norfolk, fruit from South Africa: a pity, we thought, that HM was offered no local delicacy). The lesser local notables had a lavish buffet nearby, also flown in by BOAC, salmon and all, with black brown and white guzzling together, all manners having disappeared. It was a free for all scrum, and really rather disgraceful. I also found it rather shameful the way senior officers and their wives struggled and jostled to get photographs of HM when she came out afterwards. I made a hat for myself for the occasion by taking a white African skull cap, cutting out the centre, and sewing mosquito netting over and round it. I was rather pleased with myself.

William was born on September 10th 1954. I had gone down to Entebbe to stay with the Gores who were there then, and took David with me. He was able to go to the Lake Victoria Primary School which was then very well run. Bill elected to take his time about arriving, so I was a whole month staying with Gill and Paul, and very much appreciate the way they put up with me. A heavily pregnant woman is not the liveliest of guests, and David could be a handful, but they never made me feel that I was in the way. Finally, as Bill still showed no signs of coming, I went into hospital and he was induced. When he was brought to me I was shown his very long finger nails, and told that they showed that he had been ready to come for some time before. However, once he had made his appearance Bill was a very good, untroublesome baby. He and I and David flew from Entebbe to Kasese, the airstrip for Kilembe, the copper mine in the Ruwenzori. John met us there and back we went to Fort Portal till the end of October, when we all flew to England for John's leave.

15. October 1954 — March 1955: To England and back to Fort Portal

Dick Stone, the DC (later to become PC), John, and Frank Gibson one of the ADCs had joined together in a syndicate to buy a leave car to be shared on their consecutive leaves, each contributing £50. We collected this vehicle on our arrival in

England. It was a 1936 Vauxhall, about the same size as a modern Metro, no heating of course, and with rusting cable brakes, and a hole in the floor under the front passenger's seat. In this car we went first, briefly, to Chilham where John's father had recently become the vicar, then for a short stay in Farmore where my parents had by now settled, and from there to Trebretherick in North Cornwall where we had taken a holiday cottage for two months. John and I sat in front with William on my knee, and David, Lawrence and Sally in the back — rather squashed — and in the boot William's Moses basket, a collapsible pram for him, and a push chair for Sally, and all our clothes and belongings for two months. The car was unhappy going more than about 35mph, so the journey from Hereford took a whole day. However we arrived by dark and found everything satisfactory.

The cottage, or rather a quite substantial small house, was fully furnished, including a cot for Sally, and was set on a cliff-top looking over the sea, which, there, runs into the Camel estuary. Several other holiday houses were nearby, almost all empty at this time of year, and we had the cliffs and beaches to ourselves. At low tide the sands ran a long way out into the estuary, and there on one afternoon David and Lawrence bathed in all their clothes; we couldn't believe it when we saw them bounding in the shallow waters and rushed to stop them, but by the time we got there they had come out and were standing shivering. On another occasion they took off their anoraks while playing and left them on a rock, whence the incoming tide swept them out to sea into the Bristol Channel. John used to play golf nearby, and I would take the family for walks, pushing Willie myself, and getting David to push Sally in her buggy. He amused himself by running with her over all the most bumpy places, with predictable yells from Sally. We made one or two attempts to explore Cornwall in the car, but as the braking system seized up on steep hills we were not very adventurous. The pram was parked at night, with its hood up, but no William, in a little open verandah. During a storm it started to blow away towards the cliffs, and when John went to try to rescue it he needed all his strength to wrestle with the wind, and had to hold onto the side of the house before he could drag it back to shelter.

It was a pleasant, uneventful holiday until mid-December, when we left for Chilham to spend Xmas with John's parents. The journey back took two cold days, with icy wind freezing our feet through the hole in the car's floor. We spent one night in Shaftesbury in a hotel with a fine carved dresser in the dining room. So far as I remember everybody behaved well, and despite the cold the car went well too.

The Vicarage at Chilham was a handsome Queen Anne house, with a large walled garden, outbuildings, and a servants wing attached at right angles to the rear of the main house, with living accommodation over what must have been the stables or coach house: ideal for family visits. I believe it has been sold now, and that the present vicarage is suitably semi-detached, but then the vicar was housed as his predecessors had been, if without the staff or privileges. The whole house was very cold, without proper heating, and I greatly admired John's mother for all she did. She said that being a vicar's wife was just like being a Governor's wife, but with one difference: there were very much the same chores, but no staff to help you.

The kitchen of the main house looked out along the back of our wing. One day, just as the sexton was passing below, David and Lawrence climbed out onto the window sill and pee'd down into the yard, narrowly missing him. It shows how lucky I was in my mother in law, who saw it all, that all Lady Champion said was: "You know, that could be dangerous". We had family Christmas there, and John and I took David and Lawrence to the Xmas service in the large and beautiful church. Both boys behaved very well, David in particular looking angelic as he said his prayers. But afterwards, when we got back to our quarters, he made up for it by kicking Sally's new doll's pram down the stairs.

After Christmas we again went to Farmore for a week or so. My parents seemed happy there, and were busy trying to make the old, rather dilapidated place watertight. I also saw Aunt Molly for the last time; she died shortly afterwards, and I think it was about this time also that LPJ died, aged 93.

We wanted to go out again by Aden on our way back to

Uganda. Already berths by Blue Funnel were not so easily available, but my father with his shipping connections was able to get us passages by P and O, and early in February John left the car for its next owner, and we proceeded by train to Southampton to join the *Corfu*.

This was an elderly passenger liner on her way to the Far East. We had two cabins at the bottom of the first class accommodation, just above the water line. Each cabin had a wash basin — baths and loos were at some distance. There was a cot in each cabin: one for Sally, who shared with the boys, and one for Willie who was with us. On the dressing table in our cabin was a large vase of flowers sent as an offering from the P and O management to an ex-competitor's daughter. We set sail on a rough, wet evening, and by the time we reached the Solent I felt distinctly queasy and went to lie down in my clothes. This was lucky, because by the time John, who had been invited to a quick drink with the captain before sailing, tumbled down, the ship was turning into the Channel and the full force of a severe gale, and he could only fling off his clothes onto the floor and himself, already in paroxysms, into bed. Our cabin was against a main bulkhead, so that when, almost at once, a porthole a little for'ard cracked, water poured down the corridor and flooded our cabin. At the same time a particularly violent lurch flung the vase and flowers to the floor, together with Willie and his cot, so that the flowers, and the vase, and Willie, and John's clothes (with his wallet and soaking travellers cheques) were all being swept to and fro in gallons of sea water, swish swash, from under his bunk to under mine and back again as the ship rolled, and our porthole was buried in green sea with every roll. At this point John, with real heroism, got up, pulled the cot round so that it was no longer parallel with the ship, grabbed Willie, wrapped him in blankets, and put him back in the cot. He then fell back onto his bunk, retching so terribly that I was afraid for him. At about midnight there were sounds of wailing from the cabin opposite. I forced myself up, and struggled over to find the boys sitting up saying, "What's happening?" I seized the crying Sally and took her back with me and collapsed onto my bed. I then lost all sense of time;

from time to time a gang of lascars would appear to bale out the cabin, accompanied by a kindly steward, wringing his hands amd saying, "Oh dear, what an advertisement for the P and O!". Their activity only made our sufferings worse. Fortunately the violent motion had the effect of stupefying the children, and Willie hardly woke at all. All this went on for I think about 36 hours, till we passed Gibraltar, when people gradually appeared and life returned to normal. The boys were very excited because they had seen fish in the water on the other side of their porthole.

The Mediterranean was grey but calm, and we began to make friends and eat and drink again and recount our sufferings. When I heard that the captain had fallen on the bridge and broken an arm I felt that we must have been through a proper storm, one that even my father would have appreciated. The rest of the voyage was uneventful and pleasant, and we spent a few happy days in Aden with Liz and Tom, who were then living in Khormaksar with little Jane. We had a picnic out at Little Aden, and the children scrambled up and down the large dunes. This was our last visit to Aden except for a few hours during our final voyage home in the *Europa* in 1963. I don't remember anything of the journey back to Fort Portal, but by early March we were in our house again and with the same staff. I remember Silvester telling me that I was quite thin, which was gratifying. By now Dick Stone was PC, and John the DC, but we did not move houses.

16. March — August 1955: Fort Portal and then to Entebbe

When we returned to Fort Portal we expected to spend another 18 months tour there. John had become the DC and was busy learning Lutoro, the local language. But in fact it turned out differently, much to my annoyance, as in July we were told that we were to go back to Entebbe, where John was to become AFS (Assistant Financial Secretary), a substantial promotion. Of course promotion is always agreeable, but I was just beginning to feel at home in Toro and was thoroughly enjoying safaris, so the prospect of becoming a Lady of Entebbe once more was not attractive. I remember sitting on the steps of our bungalow with a half tumbler of brandy in my hand, feeling increasingly fed up as the glass emptied. However John was naturally gratified, and what had to be had to be accepted.

During our last months in Toro I was able to go on one more safari with John on a DC's tour, walking over the mountains and down to Bundibugyo in Bwamba on the other side, and then on to Rwebisengo on the Semliki flats by Lake Albert. Mavis Stone very kindly agreed to look after Willie, while the others stayed with Joan and Frank Gibson (While we were away David, Lawrence and their friend Charlie Gibson amused themselves by letting down the tyres of guests who had come to a lunchtime party, with the doctor I think). Meanwhile our route took us over the northern flank of the Ruwenzori, to camp high up above Bundibugyo overlooking the Semliki River and the hills in the Congo beyond. It was romantic to watch the black storm clouds sweep down from the snows of the Ruwenzori behind us, and deposit their rain, first on the Semliki valley to drain down to the Nile and 3,000 miles north into the Mediterranean, and then, minutes later, on the forests, to drain 2,000 miles west down the Congo into the Atlantic Ocean.

At first the slippery path seemed as steep as the sides of a house; then, as we left cultivation and came into forest, it was only as steep as a house roof, and finally at the top of the ridge, at about 9,000ft, we were on heathy moorland which I would have liked to explore further, but there was no time, and we proceeded a little further down through forest again to our camp site, with a very fine view. We were now in the fief of Samweri Bukombi, a local notable believed to have powers of witchcraft. He had been an official Gombolola Chief and very highly regarded by successive DCs for his grip on law and order. In particular his local knowledge and expertise always enabled him to identify a thief, and he then had great success in ensuring the recovery of the stolen property — using his own methods. These consisted in constructing a pallet of bamboo poles, tying the suspect onto it, and lighting a slow fire underneath — rather like St. Lawrence on his grid. Most unfortunately on one occasion his local knowledge let him down and he got the wrong man, who indeed survived but was very severely burned. The Protectorate Authority (ie John's predecessor as DC) very properly intervened, and Samweri was now no longer a Chief. This in no way detracted from his local influence: all the official chiefs deferred to him, and he came to call on us with considerable condescension, invited us to his house, and spent several hours drinking our beer and whisky (mixed), and talking at length with us through an interpreter. This severely depleted our stock of whisky, calculated to see us through the rest of our safari.

The next day at Bundibugyo we were met by the office truck which was to take us on to Rwebisengo on the flats on the Lake Albert swampland. The driver of the truck told me with some relish that Mavis had been given a very bad cold by Willie, and was "mgonjwa sana" (very ill). We proceeded next day over rough savannah country through the elephant grass to Rwebisengo. We camped in tents amongst the worst mosquitoes I have ever encountered. The following day John had a very tricky cattle ownership case to decide, and afterwards we had tea in the Gombolola Chief's house. This time, as I sat on a cane chair, I became aware of a burning, itching sensation climbing up my legs, and realised that bugs were feasting on this unaccustomed flesh — and were moving ever higher. I wondered how long I could maintain the unconcern necessary for politeness, honour and prestige, but luckily we left before the worst happened, and I found that the itching subsided fairly fast. On our way back to Bundibugyo we were stopped by a man with a very sick child in his arms. We took them to the dispensary at Bundibugyo, but I didn't think there was much hope for the child.

I remember also a trip we did, this time with Sally as a baby in her basket, when in the evening, on our way between two Gombololas, our car and the truck containing all our kit got stuck in the mud at the bottom of a steep, hill. Drums were beaten (a sort of local tocsin), all the locals were summoned and got our car, but not the truck, up the hill as it got dark,and we spent a very uncomfortable night in a small tent on the half flooded playground of the local primary school, crowded in with Sally, unfed (though there was a bit of whisky left in the bottle), and trying to beat off the mosquitoes.

During those last few months in Fort Portal David and Lawrence were able to go to an English primary school which had been started in a rondavel hut on the site of the old fort, near the club. Aided and abetted by his buddy the policeman's son, during break one day David succeeded in locking the teacher and all the rest of her class into the single room of the school, and then taunted them from outside. This was not very well received. Another of his achievements, with Lawrence this time, was to set fire to Sarapio's house and burn his bedding and his few clothes. We had been out to dinner, and came back to find a considerable disturbance. Sarapio was, understandably, extremely indignant. However he cheered up a good deal when he realised that we were going to replace everything, and that he would be getting a complete new outfit. The next day I went down to the local shopkeeper, Jeraj, a very pleasant Ismaili, and arranged for Sarapio to choose selected garments. Afterwards, when he heard the story, Jeraj said, "Madam, I am thinking you have very naughty children".

One other memory of Fort Portal is worth recording. A colony of bees was living in the roof of our bungalow. We came home one evening from some party to a wild and savage scene. Great flickering torches of tarred stakes were waving about; Kiiza with an axe was wrenching the corrugated iron roof from its supports; angry and smoky bees were flying confusedly around; Polito was standing on a stool on the verandah, plunging his bare arms up to the elbows into the bees nest and pulling out and filling a basin with great hunks of wax and honey and bees, casually flicking bees off himself and picking stings out of his arms as he did so. We had some of the honey next day. It was very good: strong, a bit smoky, and you had to watch out for the bees.

17. August 1955 — October 1956: Entebbe

We went down to Entebbe early in August, and settled into a house in Mugula Road, a new development overlooking the airport. Lawrence was able to go to the Entebbe Primary School which was either then or a little later very well run by David Price Hughes, but our David was due to start at St. Bedes, Eastbourne, in September. Tony Champion had taught there and said it was the best school of its kind that he knew, and kind Ken de Torre whom we had met and liked in Grantown was the sports master there. So at the end of August Dave and I went back to England by air. John was distressed at the parting, but David was happy and excited. On the flight home we were delayed for 24 hours in Cairo, and taken by BOAC to look at the pyramids. David escaped from the party and ran ahead up inside the steep passage; he passed us coming down as we reached the top, and I wondered if I would find him again, but luckily he had had the sense to wait for us.

In England we went to stay at Farmore and were taken for drives by my father. We also stayed for a few days with my brother David who had a flat in Eaton Terrace, and who took us to the Tower. DSC was in his new grey flannel school uniform, jacket, shorts and socks, and as we were standing in a long queue waiting to see the crown jewels his childish, clear voice proclaimed, "Christ, it's fucking, bloody hot". Basic English was not so commonplace then as it is now, and the queue fell silent. I replied, "Well, take your coat off then" — which he did. My brother leant down and congratulated me on David's remarkable command of

79

language. I confess that I was surprised myself, but put it down to association with Michael Perry, son of the policeman at Fort Portal, Doug Perry. We went dowm to Eastbourne by train, and by taxi to St. Bedes. David had beem quite chirpy all the way, but when we reached the school he refused to get out of the taxi, and the driver and I had to lift him out between us. It was painful, but I then took him in without further trouble, and left him resolutely. If something unpleasant has to be done the way to do it is to face it, take a deep breath, and get on with it as fast and as firmly as you can.

Boarding schools are the subject of much opprobrium from the present 'politically correct' brigade, and indeed if I lived near a good day school now I would not send my children away — where would be the point, quite apart from any question of expense? But in Uganda in the 50s if one's children were to have any chance of higher education later they had to go away. Some indeed went to Kenya, but already by 1955 the future there seemed uncertain, and in any case one wanted one's young to be formed in our own British rather than in a colonial cultural heritage, as in similar circumstances John had been. So like nearly all our contemporaries we sent our children away to school in England when they were about eight or nine. There were boarding school allowances from the Government to help with the fees, and each child was entitled to one free holiday air passage each year; sometimes we paid for an extra air passage ourselves. Later some of ours spent some of their other holidays at Chagford in Devon, where Mrs Watkinson, the widow of a senior civil engineer who was lost when the submarine *Thetis* sank on her trials in 1939 just before the outbreak of the war, kept a holiday home. To judge from some of the stories of those holidays which we heard later, she had a demanding task. St. Bedes was a success for David. When he came out the following summer he called John 'Sir', and me 'Matron' for the first 24 hours, but then he was again the merry scamp he had always been, and he never minded going back to school.

I went back to Entebbe after leaving David, and settled back into a familiar but slightly different way of life. We had been able to save some money while in Fort Portal, and so, in addition to our red and grey Morris Oxford Estate car (a very good one: the black Standard Vanguard had not been a success), we bought ourselves a little green Morris Minor convertible, which was great fun for us to drive, and for the children too, piled into the rear. Sheba was still with us, and still producing puppies in large numbers. We kept one of them, the fruit of a deliberate attempt at a black labrador cross, but he turned out to be completely untrainable, and a dog expert afterwards told me one should never attempt a backwards cross. Eventually he ran out in front of a car and was killed.

Silvester, Polito and Kiiza were all there, and of course Jeneti too. Sarapio came down with us to Entebbe, but then went to work for someone else. We also had Rwakasenyi as garden boy. He was the laziest person we ever employed: half an hour pushing a mower in the morning and half an hour in the evening was all he ever did — except drink. This made it particularly galling for John, delighted with his new promotion (which put him on £2,000 a year), when Lawrence, then at five a fierce radical, asked me how much we paid Rwakasenyi. I told him (it was not much). "And how much does Daddy get?" I told him — it was rather more. "But that's not fair: Rwakasenyi works much harder than Daddy!". A few months later we moved to a larger house and garden, 49 Circular Road, where we stayed for the rest of our time in Uganda. Then we had to get rid of Rwakasenyi because the rest of our staff insisted, and Yowana came to take his place, a really good worker.

Catherine was born on 23 May 1956. From the very earliest days she was admirable, as she has remained ever since: never has there been a less troublesome baby. The children kept me busy; we spent much time at the swimming pool, or playing on the beach, or walking in the Botanic gardens and at the far end of the Entebbe peninsula where there was some forest and a swamp where you could see interesting birds. John was busy at work; he was responsible for drafting the Protectorate budget, but also found plenty of time for golf, and became quite good at it, with a single figure handicap. The usual social life went on. I don't remember so much of the Hard Core: some had now left, and perhaps we were all getting older. However there was the Entebbe Dramatic Society. Acting has never been one of my strong points, so I was content to watch John cavorting on the boards. We played quite a lot of bridge in the evenings: jolly bridge, not too serious, with reckless bids and much laughter at the resulting disasters — a bad practise for a much later attempt at competition bridge in aid of charity in Hereford when we experienced massive humiliations, never to be repeated voluntarily. I also started to learn Luganda seriously, and by the time we left in 1963 I was beginning to feel that I had made the breakthrough — alas all to be wasted.

18. October 1956 — February 1957: To England and Back

We flew home in early October, just before the Suez crisis — luckily, as it would not have been agreeable to get delayed in Cairo. We had booked a holiday cottage in Thorpeness on the Suffolk coast, and also hired a car, hoping to explore Norfolk and Suffolk, and visit the many fine churches. This was not to be, as petrol rationing was already in force by the time John collected the car. In applying for petrol coupons he was advised by the helpful assistant in the AA office to state our leave destination as Wick or Thurso in order to acquire the maximum possible number of coupons, and as a result we were able to allow ourselves one or two excursions, but on the whole we found ourselves pretty tightly restricted.

However after a few days at Chilham we drove without problems up to Thorpeness with Lawrence, Sally, Willie and baby Catherine, and settled happily into a small semi-detached former fisherman's cottage by the sea. There was a small golf course near a prominent windmill for John, and a large artificial lake with lots of waterfowl which the children enjoyed. The beach was flat, shingle and pebbles and dull, stretching north and south the same for miles. About 1½ — 2 miles to the north of our house there was a low cliff, the Ness I suppose. John played golf, while I pushed the baby buggy round the heath as the children romped ahead, and we walked along the cold, unfriendly November beach. I'm sure it is very different in August, but it was not enticing then. In the evenings we read Noddy stories to the children (unexpurgated), and other improving works. There was no TV of course, and no-one any the worse for that. My brother David who was then working in London came for a few days, and also Liz and Jane. While David was with us and we were walking along the beach, John tried to demonstrate the art of backward somersaults at which he had once considered himself expert. He managed one, just, but the second attempt doubled him up in agony, and that was the end: at 35 he realised that he was getting old. Our David came for the holidays and we spent Christmas there; cooking the turkey in an old, small electric cooker was something of a challenge, but it worked. However the other episode from that Xmas which I remember was not so successful. Lawrence had been a particular fan of the Noddy stories, so I thought, foolishly, that he would like a large, floppy toy Big Ears. How little I understood a six year old boy! He gave it one indignant look and flung it furiously from him; too late I realised what an insult it was to him.

But the most memorable event of that leave was the disappearance of Willie, then aged two years and four months. Whenever I think of it I recognise how lucky we all were that he was found. In the mornings when it was fine the children would go to play on the beach, which was only a few yards from the house, while I did the minimum necessary cleaning and nappy washing. One day, early in January, I went out after my chores to collect them — and there was no Willie. A swift search around showed no sign of him, and the beach was empty for half a mile or more in each direction, north and south. So, increasingly anxious, we searched in wider and wider circles, as far as the pond — could he have fallen in? ...the golf course?... was he lost on the heath?.... the shops?.... had he been run over?.... or kidnapped... and so on. At last it was lunch time, and by now I was getting desperate, but didn't want to show this to the other children. So we decided that I would produce food in the normal way, while John would go to the Police (we had no telephone). Just as he was going out to do so a man approached from the house opposite: "Had we lost a small child? There had been a telephone message from the big house beyond the cliff to say that one had been found by a fisherman, walking along the beach northwards towards Lowestoft, and was now in their kitchen". What a relief! John got in the car and went off the two miles to collect Willie, whom he found, silent but self-possessed, in the great kitchen of the local manor, surrounded by kindly domestic staff with whom he did not know how to communicate. He was brought back, apparently quite unaware of anything unusual having happened — but he did go to sleep while I was pushing him over the heath that afternoon. Later, when I dried off his outdoor suit, I found a piece of melted chocolate in one of the pockets.

Shortly after this we left Thorpeness and went down to Chilham again, spending a night with Jean and Henry Hobbs in Richmond on the way. We had wanted to take David and Lawrence to a pantomime in London, but did not like to leave the other small and demanding children with John's mother who had plenty to do anyway. So, recommended by Hazel Morris and Ann Greenwood, we tried the St. Julian's Childrens Home near Horsham, a C of E establishment run by 'kind ladies.' We had no complaints to make when we collected the children afterwards, but the régime was strict, and Sally tells another story.

Finally we went to Farmore. It was wintry weather, and I remember our first walk up Garway Hill, taken there by my brother Stopford, who was also visiting. We walked up through thin and slippery snow on a very murky afternoon. David and Lawrence threw snowballs and slid about, and David pushed Lawrence over on a frozen puddle and made him cry. But the important feature of this Hereford visit was

Copper Beeches

our decision to buy Copper Beeches. It was becoming
obvious that we needed to have a permanent base in England
to which we could come on leave, and which the children
could regard as home. Also, as the Suez débacle had shown,
our position in the world was no longer secure, and we had to
be prepared for uncertainty and change — and where better
to face it than from one's own place? Besides, with the
increasing size of our family, rented holiday accommodation
on leave was becoming more and more expensive, and it was
not fair to expect grandparents always to put us all up either.
Across the field from Farmore was Copper Beeches, a small
house built in the 30s, two up and two down, with a pleasant
garden, a bit of wood and a fine view over to Wales and the
Black Mountains. It was on the market, and we bought it in
early 1957 at the very end of our leave for £4,500. While we
were away on the following tour we had it enlarged by two
small rooms upstairs and one large one down for a further

£1,300. My mother kept an eye on the work while we were away, and when we next came on leave, in 1958, it was waiting for us, and remained a happy and welcoming second home for us all until 1976.

19. January 1957 — October 1958: Entebbe

The Suez episode, revealing as it had our weakness in the face of American hostility and the continuous Russian attempts at subversion, made it clear to the intelligent politician that the Colonial Empire was becoming unsustainable. In fact the writing had been on the wall ever since India achieved her independence in 1948. The West African colonies, starting with Ghana in 1956, were already on their way to independence, and events in East Africa such as the Mau Mau rebellion were all pointing in the same direction. Although Macmillan's celebrated 'Wind of Change' speech did not take place till 1959, preliminary breezes were beginning to be felt in Uganda by 1957. However it is worth noting that several of the most senior officials even then did not accept that it was happening. Indeed less than eighteen months before it did the then Chief Secretary assured his European staff that their jobs in Uganda were safe for some years yet to come.

The Kabaka had returned from exile, I think in 1956, and there was a rather embarrassing Government House Garden Party for the Queen's birthday to which of course he had to be invited (and at which he behaved with the greatest suavity) by Andrew Cohen who had deported him, and who was replaced as Governor early in 1957 by Sir Frederick Crawford. As part of the attempt to introduce Westminster type government selected Africans were now being appointed to minor ministerial posts, among them Kironde, Minister of

49 Circular Rd, Entebbe

Public Works,who lived behind us in Mugula Road. Lawence became very friendly with his eldest son of the same age, Kadu. The Entebbe swimming pool was, of course still reserved for Europeans, and this meant that Laurie could not go there with Kadu. They played happily together on the shallow sandy beach on Lake Victoria by the airport, but Laurie enjoyed swimming and diving, and said to me one day, "Mum, who made the swimming pool?" I had a fairly good idea of what was behind this, so started to fudge the issue: "Well, the Europeans thought that they would like to have a pool, so they got together in a club and collected the money to build it and..." At this Lawrence came straight to the point: "But who did the work? Was it Europeans or Africans?" " Africans I suppose". "Then why can't they use it?" I had no answer.

At about this time we moved from Mugula Road to 49 Circular Road, where we lived for the rest of our time in

Uganda. This was a large, old style bungalow, with two central rooms leading off a verandah, and one large and one small bedroom on each side with bathrooms attached. The kitchen quarters were at the back, and beyond them the staff quarters. There was a large garden in which I vainly tried to grow roses, but Yowana was successful with French beans at the back, and we did plant, and finally left flourishing, a cassia tree in the central circle of the driveway. We also had some splendid amaryllis. A big mango tree grew outside our bedroom, and a mulberry tree and an avocado behind. On one occasion a nest of flying ants swarmed and broke through a crack in the polished concrete floor of our bedroom. These were a great African delicacy, and when Sylvesta brought us our early morning tea and saw them he put down our tray and started eating them at once, live, off the wing. The floor then had to be dug right up, and the Queen found (and eaten) before the nest could be cleared. Neither John nor I ever ate ants, but the children did; they said they tasted like butter. Another delicacy which I enjoyed was the local grasshopper, which swarmed in November around the street lights. The Africans came in groups to collect them, and they were then fried and eaten rather like whitebait: very good I thought, but John was too conservative to bring himself to try them. There were also tiny mushrooms which appeared from time to time on the golf course and made very good soup. Even the unenterprising John was prepared to have a go at this. However on one occasion when we were half way through the soup I realised that the little black things in it were not mushrooms but grasshopper eyes; I wondered if John was going to notice. He did! One delicacy which we all loved was ngege, the local Lake Victoria carp, tasty, rather like plaice. I believe it has now been almost entirely exterminated by giant Nile Perch, introduced into the lake from the Nile by some well meaning international aid organisation seeking to provide a new major source of protein; it was the predatory perch which got the protein at the expense of the unhappy and delicious ngege. There's a moral to this story, I suspect.

In September of this year our third daughter, Diana, was born. Had we been in England she might have survived, but as it was, with a hole in her heart and no special care facilities, she only lived for a few hours. I knew at once that there was something wrong, as she was taken away and I was put in a room by myself. Although I try hard not to be superstitious yet I have sometimes wondered whether there was any significance in the fact that I lay awake listening to the nearby church clock striking the quarters, and went to sleep after hearing it strike 2am, and then, on Diana's death certificate, the time of death given was 0210. She was buried under a cypress in the Kampala cemetery. Pat and Selwyn Few were there, and were very kind to John who carried the little box in his arms. As for myself, I found I minded less than the other time: as you get older you learn how to bear misfortune, your own and others', with more resignation and fortitude, and so are less inadequate at helping others to bear their share.

Meanwhile John was kept very busy as AFS, responsible for the drafting of the annual Protectorate budget, and at the New Year of 1958 he decided to take some well-earned local leave and go down to the Kenya coast. In order to get the maximum time away we left Entebbe on New Years Day, a public holiday and Lawrence's 8th birthday. Let it be a warning to other innocent but thoughtless parents that I doubt even now whether Lawrence has forgiven us for (a) having fried eggs for breakfast, which I knew he didn't like, and (b) for making him carsick all the long car journey to Kaptagat in the Kenya Highlands where we spent the night. However once we got to the coast the holiday was a great success for all, except perhaps Willie. While we were away Catherine and Jeneti stayed with the Fews, whose son William was about Catherine's age, but we thought that Willie, who had so much loved playing on the beach by the shores of Lake Victoria would also love the sea. But we were mistaken: the whole time we were there he screamed hysterically whenever we took him near the water. Years later he told us that he had been terrified of the tiny hermit crabs which were everywhere burrowing about in the sand.

I cannot remember the name of the holiday camp where we stayed. It was a few miles north of Mombasa, very simple African style huts, with rows of ablutions behind them and a central dining area and bar. Palm trees waved around, and the sea was barely 100 yards away, quite safe bathing as there was a reef beyond the lagoon to keep out the sharks. In the evening John and I would walk along the deserted silver beach in the moonlight, listening to the waves breaking on the reef. 30 years later, when Sally and Catherine went on a holiday to Kenya,it was unsafe to go out at night, and by day they were continually being pestered by young local male prostitutes, corrupted by female, especially Germanic, tourists.

I remember two other episodes, apart from Willie and the crabs: — when David was stung by a Portuguese Man of War (a peculiarly vicious jelly fish), and when a bird-eating spider settled on Sally's mosquito net. On both these occasions John showed the same calm good sense that he did in other emergencies. While I stood staring at David, aged 10, who was speechless and quivering with pain, John picked up a wodge of wet sand and swept the tentacles off his chest; and secondly, while I fled to the corner of our hut at the sight of this spider, the size of a man's fist, John knocked it off the net and caught it in Sally's toy doll's carry basket, put a paper on top and threw it out of the window. At the first attempt it jumped back into the room and hid on the underside of Sally's cot. John had to get down on his back on the floor to knock it off and catch it again, but this time it was thrown out properly and disappeared into the night. We never saw it again. Under her net Sally was quite unalarmed throughout the whole performance.

On the way back John had to stay back in Nairobi on some official business, so I set off in the red and grey Morris with the children to drive in a day the 300 miles to Jinja to spend the night with Joan and Frank Gibson. All was well till beyond Nakuru where the tarmac ran out and the road was only metalled. As we started to climb through the forest towards Mau Summit one of the tyres punctured and we slid into the side of the road. David and I had had a lesson in wheel changing so we set to work, but with the car at a slope we were not getting on very far, when a solitary African carrying a panga (machete) came up the road. The Mau Mau rising had then only very recently been put down, and fear clutched me when I saw him. However you must never show it, so I said, "Jambo. Wewe naweza kusaidia mimi?" — terrible pidgin Swahili for "Hullo. Can you help me?" This he did quite amiably, and we set off again with him in the car for a few miles. When he got out I thanked him most warmly and gave him five shillings — about £15 now — which pleased him. We went on to Eldoret where I had the tyre repaired in a Sikh garage, so it was nearly dark when we finally reached Jinja.

The rest of the tour passed uneventfully. Lawrence was being very well taught by David Price Hughes, and Sally had started at the kindergarten run by Alison Coutts. Alison and her husband Pip, a colleague of John's were our next door neighbours — and Pip's father had been one of John's grandfather's protegés in the Scottish kirk in Glasgow. Sally and Trina Coutts were good friends, and Lawrence and Conky (Alastair) Coutts, with Ian Burgess and later Dougy Badger were mischievous together. David joined in during the holidays. There were two gangs: one, the Mighty Eagles, was led by Conky Coutts; the other, the Pear Balls, so called from the rotten avocados, windfalls from our tree, which were used by both sides as missiles, was led by David. I never knew the full details, but apparently on one occasion Lawrence betrayed the Pear Balls to the Mighty Eagles, was unmasked, and was lucky not to suffer the fate of Tarpeia.

20. October 1958 — May 1960: Copper Beeches and Entebbe

We went back to England on leave in the autumn of 1958, and at the same time Lawrence joined David at St. Bedes. After a visit to Chilham we went down to Hereford with a hired car and started life in Copper Beeches, which soon became 'home' for us all. We made expeditions to the Black

91

Mountains, Garway Hill, and the Queen's Wood (ideal for small children), and began to learn about south Herefordshire. I remember three things particularly about this time: firstly, for almost six weeks there was continuous cloud and mist; secondly, John was afflicted for the first time by a series of boils and carbuncles which almost turned him into another Job; and thirdly, when the vicar, the Revd. Leathley, called unannounced on a pastoral visit at tea time, Sally locked us all into the dining room, and John had to climb awkwardly through the hatch to release us. I took Sally, shrieking but *not* chastised upstairs, but her yells could be heard below, and the vicar remarked to John: "It is sometimes hard to temper justice with mercy"!

Tony and June Champion came to stay with us for a few days after Christmas, bringing Tim with them, and I remember a walk with them up Garway Hill in the snow. There was also a Christmas tea party at Farmore on my mother's birthday, on December 28. Altogether it was a happy and restful few months — except for John and his boils.

We went back to Uganda in January, and shortly afterwards John had a small promotion and was appointed Acting Permanent Secretary in the Ministry of Health, the job he enjoyed the most of all he had in Uganda. His Minister was Sir John Croot, a distinguished Professor of surgery, whose operations had included the removal of a bunion from my right foot. When John started to work for him, he had had no recollection of me whatsoever, but a little later, when we invited him over for a picnic lunch by the swimming pool, he suddenly recognised, and seized and started to wiggle my big toe with great self-satisfaction: "Did I do that? It's very nice! Look how mobile it is!" Bill Davies was Director of Medical Services, and he and John worked well together, and we got to know and like him and Joan very much. It was an exciting time to be in the Ministry of Health: the Uganda Government, with British Development Aid, was in the process of building what was to be at that time the largest hospital south of the Sahara excluding South Africa itself, as the teaching hospital for the whole region. The knowledge and understanding of doctors and their ways

92

which John acquired at this time was to be a great help to him much later, in the 80s.

As Independence was by now accepted as inevitable by nearly everyone, there was a great drive at most levels towards greater social and racial integration; in fact this had now become 'politically correct'. One of the movements started with this object was the Uganda Council of Women — a sort of local version of the Womens Institute. I remember going to tea parties at which select Asian, African and European women all collected in their separate groups, and senior officials' wives (I wasn't quite one yet) went from one group to another trying to persuade us to fraternise — or perhaps, in order to placate feminists, I should say 'sororize'. It wasn't very successful, but there were various attached activities, one of which I much enjoyed. A group of Baganda women out at Old Entebbe wanted to learn English, so I wemt out to teach them. I learned more Luganda than they did English, but I did have one success. We had a complete set of the Little Black Sambo books which I took out, and which proved immensely popular. They especially liked 'Little Black Mingo' as they could relate better to the familiar crocodile than to tigers. We had much laughter at it all. What rubbish to ban these books as racist — and what an insult it is to Africans and other black people to treat them in this way like silly children!

By now I was becoming quite fluent in Luganda, along certain well worn tracks. The Red Cross ran a weekly baby clinic in the local hospital under the auspices of UNICEF, and I went along as interpreter; that is to say, I asked the mothers a series of set questions in Luganda and recorded the answers in English. Most of our clients were Baganda, but the policemen's wives were nearly all Acholi from the Northern Province. If they knew no pidgin Swahili communication with them was difficult, so Betty Boyd, one of the most senior ladies, whose husband had been Provincial Commissioner in the north, learnt off the questions in Acholi. She never understood the answers, but being a lady of vast experience had no difficulty in recording them. I sometimes wondered about the strict accuracy of the statistical returns we sent off to UNICEF and thence to the

World Health Organisation, but about this time John's office received a very complimentary letter from WHO Headquarters in Rome on their comprehensive quality.

Peter was born on July 30, 1959. All my babies were large — two, Lawrence and Catherine, over 10lbs, and even Sally the smallest was 8½ lbs. Peter was 9lbs, 15ozs. As I have short legs, towards the end of each pregnancy I looked like a barrel on two little stumps, and was well aware of this. Shortly before Peter arrived I was shopping in Figueiredo's store when I heard one of two small African boys, about 11, say to the other: *"Lab' omukyala oyo — ng' alina lubuto!"* ("Look at that woman, what a belly she's got on her!"), so I replied: *"Kyamazima"*, which means 'That's dead right', and was delighted to have them squeal *"Ee-ee-ee"* ('Cor Blimey!'), and run giggling from the shop. One of the pleasures of learning Luganda was to be able to join unexpectedly in the surrounding conversation in shops, markets and elsewhere.

Peter flourished and was no trouble at this stage. In October, I think, my mother came out for a visit with my uncle Stopford and Aunt Kate, and also Aunt Alice. They stayed in the Lake Victoria Hotel, by now quite a good standard tourist hotel, and made a tour of Toro, Kigezi and the game park, from which my mother brought back some fine photographs. It was lovely to see them, as I know they enjoyed coming out. I am glad that we were able to provide them with an opportunity to see Uganda at what seems now to have been one of its best and happiest stages.

John made several tours with John Croot, including one to the Northern Province, and after Christmas when David and Lawrence were both on holiday, we decided to take a local leave in Karamoja. Karamoja is in the extreme north east corner of Uganda, bordering the Turkana country of Kenya and what was known as 'the terrible Rudolph region', that is, the wild and barren land round Lake Rudolph. The Karamojong, the least sophisticated of all the tribes in Uganda, were nomadic cattle people whose national sport was cattle raiding. In our time they practised this sport only with their long, 7ft fighting spears, but later, in the chaos which followed Amin, they acquired Kalashnikovs, with which in the pursuit of cattle and booty they massacred and devastated all around them, particularly the fertile, settled district of Teso to their west and south. Only now (1992) are conditions just beginning to improve. The District HQ was Moroto, lying beneath a large mountain mass. Further south, towards the border with Mbale and Mount Elgon a dramatic fang-like mountain, Debasien or Kadam of which more later, rose from the plain. The Karamojong warrior, all six or more feet of him, wore nothing at all except a short black cloak like an oxford commoner's gown on his back, a pair of sandals made out of old tyre rubber, and a brightly painted head dress of plastered mud and cow-dung to denote his age group and status in the clan — and of course his formidable spear. To wear trousers, he believed, would compromise his manhood. The Baganda, a particularly modest people in matters of dress, considered them total savages, and when I told Jeneti of our plans to go there she was very disapproving. However, leaving the others behind with friends, and Jeneti and Peter, who was by now weaned, with the Gibsons in Mbale, we duly set off.

We had warned David and Laurie that the men where we were going wore no clothes, and that there was nothing odd about that, but they still found it curious, and when we crossed the border into Karamoja from Teso and met a herdsman with his cattle who wrapped his cloak round him against the dust from the car, David leant out of the window and shouted 'Coward!' at him. Luckily he didn't understand. We stayed in the rest house at Moroto, and had a bathe in the local pool, a mud bath with frogs in it. We also made a day tour of the surrounding country, scrubby, arid grassland, much overgrazed but still wild. In the evening John shot a guinea fowl which we had for supper. The next day we made the ascent of Imajit, one of the side peaks of Mt. Moroto at 10.116ft. We had as guides a local chap wearing his national dress (that is, virtually nothing), and an office boy to carry the three water bottles between the six of us, and some boiled sweets — not enough as we found later. We climbed up through scrubby forest to a grassy ridge and from there a long pull up to the summit. David bounded along, but Lawrence, then just 10, needed some emcouragement. When we reached the top there was a fine view down over the plains, and just below us the tiny houses of Moroto. "Is that where we're going?" said Lawrence, "well I can't". "Well then", I said, "you'll have to stay here". He saw the point, and after we'd drunk the water and eaten the sweets we set off down again. We had no common language with our guide, but the office boy had Swahili, and told us that there was a particular thorn tree with medicinal fruit that the guide wanted to get for his child, and that there would be a slight detour. This turned out to take two hours in the hottest part of the day, round the northern flank of the ridge through the scrubby forest. We all became very thirsty; Laurie plodded on in silence, but David became increasingly mutinous, and said things about the guide which I'm glad he did not understand. However at last we reached the tree, and it was worth it all to see the guide climbing up it. I never found out its name, but it was of medium size, covered all over with large sharp thorns, and with the berries hanging outwards over the edge of a steep slope. He climbed, quite naked except for the cloak behind him and his sandals, out along an overhanging branch among the thorns, and collected a quantity of fruit which was put with the now empty water bottles. Then at last we could go back. When we reached the rest house we had to pay off the guide and the office boy, shake them by the hands, thank them and say what a great day it had been, almost voiceless with thirst, and then at last retreat and drink our fill.

After this we went back to the civilised world of Entebbe. The boys went back to school, and life continued uneventfully until May, when John was appointed Permanent Secretary for Security and External Relations — another promotion. (Later the job was found to be too much for one man and was redesignated Internal Affairs).

During this time there were two changes in our household. Polito was taken queer while cooking our Xmas dinner — I think it's called having a little turn', ie a slight stroke. He recovered and then went home to Toro, with a present from us, and we later heard that he was well settled in his retirement. Paulo, who had been cook for Paul and Gill Gore, who had gone to Mauritius, came in his place and stayed till we left. Reliable and humorous, he made delicious fish curry, and grasshopper soup as well. And secondly, one morning Lawrence came in to us and said, "Mum, Sheba's dead, and ants are all over her nose". She had been failing for some time, so it was no surprise. She was buried in the vegetable patch at the back, and Lawrence made a memorial to her on a wooden plank:

SHEBA, THE FAITHFUL OLD DOG
OF THE CHAMPION FAMILY
1950 – 1960
MOTHER OF 96

This lasted till just the time we left in 1963, by which time the ants had started to consume it: '*Tout passe; tout casse.*'

21. May 1960 — April 1961
The Congo crisis and others

When it became clear that Independence was coming soon steps were taken to reduce the number of European civil servants and what was called the '45 Rule' was introduced. This meant that officers aged 45 and over could take early retirement with pension and redundancy money. As this was a time of full U.K. economic expansion both at home and overseas all the competent senior officers took advantage of the opportunity and resigned, thereby opening good prospects for their juniors. This was how John, at 39, achieved one of the most demanding and interesting posts in the service. Within a month of his promotion the Congo blew up and he was put to the test.

I cannot remember all the details of the Congo Independence fiasco but they will be well recorded elsewhere. From our point of view it meant that within a few days of

97

Independence early in June, Belgian settlers, officials and businessmen with their families came pouring by the car load into Uganda leaving all their belongings behind. Large groups, particularly around what was then called Stanleyville found themselves isolated, surrounded by warring Congolese factions, and an international air lift, operating from Uganda, had to be organised to rescue them. I also remember at some time a contingent of Ethiopian troops (Haile Selassie was still Emperor) under U.N. auspices passing through Entebbe airport on their way to some 'peace keeping' operation. For about 3 weeks John hardly came home at all and when he did the telephone rang constantly, sleep was only possible for brief intervals. Sally and I both remember the unexpected visit of a senior Belgian official from the area bordering on Kigezi whom John brought home one evening, we practised our very rusty French on him, he was very courteous. Large groups of these refugees were quartered in the Lake Victoria Hotel while awaiting air transport, in very elderly Constellations, back to Belgium. As I was involved in the Red Cross I was not surprised to be rung up from the Kampala H.Q. (bureaucracy at work again), to say that they were concerned that not enough was being done to help the women refugees and so I found myself lumbered with a consignment of several dozen sanitary towels to be distributed when needed. So I put them in a large African basket and took them to the hotel where men, women and children and the media were all milling around. They all crowded round me so I said "Est-ce qu'il y a une dame qui a besoin de ceci?" They poked and prodded and then one said "Ah c'est la bande hygienique", another said, "C'est pour après l'accouchement", another "Pour moi c'est fini". I left the basket and its contents and went back to 49 Circular Road. I heard no more about it.

The pressure lasted for about two months and then life in Uganda returned to normal. We had been hoping to make a trip up Mt. Elgon with the boys in their summer holidays but were not able to arrange it. However, Pip Coutts and George Badger (a forestry officer, Dougy's father), were going with Conky and Doug up Mt. Kadam on the Karamoja border and we were able to join them. The ascent involved 2 nights in camp and a team of naked porters were waiting for us at the starting point with a guide, distinctive by the fact that he wore an old burberry type macintosh and nothing else. It was raining but not the whole time and we had a beautiful night in camp on the first spur followed by a long day to the final ascent, going up and down through forest along a very muddy track. However, by the time we reached the final ascent it was getting late and it was obvious that we were not going to make the summit and back to camp before dark. So reluctantly we had to turn back, much to David's indignation as he was going very well with the advance guide and would easily have made it. On the way back I slipped crossing a stream and sat up to my waist in very cold water much to the general amusement of both black and white.

Some time before this we had acquired a little dinghy, with a single sail, which we kept on the beach out at Buku point where there was also a jetty and a rescue launch for the airport manned by 2 jovial Africans who never had much to do. David and Lawrence went out in this quite often, they never became skilled with the sail, but they were quite handy with the oars and used to go fishing in the lake. One day I had gone down in the car to fetch them home for lunch and there they were, a few 100 yards out, fishing away. I called and shouted but there was no response, one of the boat crew came and stood with me and joked, I was just getting annoyed when suddenly a hippo put its head out of the water quite near the boat. Instantly it was as though the boat had acquired wings, it shot through the water the oars whizzing. The African rocked with laughter and I felt gratified.

A more alarming adventure took place later, I think probably in the Xmas holidays of 1960 – 61. David and William Morris had gone out in the boat and sailed across the channel to the opposite side, about 2 – 3 miles. Then they did not know how to tack back and tried to row but could not make it against the wind and water so they were stranded on a mud bank. As before I went to fetch them in the car and looked around — there was no sign of them. I was becoming anxious when the boatman came again and explained what had happened and pointed to where they were — too far to see. So I went home and fetched John and Henry Morris and

99

we wondered what to do. Luckily Tommy Gee had quite a large boat which he also kept at Buku and he came down and very gallantly went across and rescued the boys and towed back the boat. We were so glad to see them that there were no recriminiations. About October 1960, as part of the process towards Independence it was decided to hold elections. There were 3 parties the U.P.C. (Uganda People's Congress) led by Milton Obote, a semi-Socialist party drawing most of its support from northern districts, the Democratic Party led by Benedicto Kiwanuka, basically a Catholic party, and the Kabaka Yekka (Only the Kabaka), which as its name implies was exclusively Baganda supported, and which aimed at separate independence for Buganda. I cannot remember the details but the UPC decided to boycott the elections (as being not sufficiently liberal), the Kabaka Yekka declared U.D.I. and left the Democratic Party which naturally won that election and Bênedicto Kiwanuka became Chief Minister in rather the same way as George Kalsakau did later in the New Hebrides. In order to make it quite clear to the Baganda that they weren't going to be allowed to get away with it a battalion of the KAR (King's African Rifles) from Kenya were brought in to march in full battle order through Kampala with the local KAR. This was effective and although there was another total boycott of Asian shops and Protectorate activities there was no serious trouble. I remember John and others being rather disparaging about Freddy Crawford over reacting but the fact remains that by anticipating trouble he had prevented it. Lady Crawford had died, I think in 1959, and as hostess in Government House her sister had come to help. She was Greek and at that time probably in her mid-to-late 50s. I remember going to a G.H. dinner party during this time when the Sudanese ambassador, an intelligent and humorous Afro/Arab was the guest of honour. Towards the end of the meal a long column of safari ants swarmed up on to the polished table and over and down by the hostess's side. The ambassador, whose name I have forgotten, leant over to her and said in his dark, fruity voice, "Ants like sweet things", not bad I thought. The only other episode I remember connected with this time was when two young and attractive KAR officers came to stay with us while arranging for their later intervention, Sally, aged seven flirted with them quite remarkably only to be equalled by Catherine with Fred Rosier in '62. In February 1961 I was rung from the office with the news that my father had died aged 78. As I later heard he had had a slight stroke and had been put to bed and told to stay there. But the following day he felt better, refused to stay in bed and came down for lunch and a large glass of South African sherry — his usual habit. After lunch he went to get himself a cigar and on the way, below the stairs, fell down dead. A shock for my Mother, though not entirely unexpected, but a good end for him. His last years in Farmore had been very happy and I am glad he did not live to be disabled and wretched. In early March my mother came out for a few weeks and shortly after she left we followed for three months' leave.

22. April 1961 — September 1962
Copper Beeches — Entebbe — Copper Beeches

We had 3 months happy leave, hiring a car we made many journeys into Wales both the Black Mountains and into Radnorshire and in the spring and summer got to know the country better. William Morris, who had just gone to Cheltenham, came to spend the Easter holidays with us and he and David got up to various misdemeanours such as digging up cats' eyes from the road and making catapult assaults on the windows of Mrs. Lloyd's caravan. Luckily they got away with it. During the term Sally, Willy and Catherine all went to the local school at Bullinghope. They walked down to Johnson's garage and caught the bus to the Bullinghope turn, walked up to school and reversed home in the afternoon. They made several friends and began to acquire Hereford accents. After the Congo débacle we began to consider the possibilities of something similar happening in Uganda and decided it would be safer to send Sally to school in England. So we arranged for her to go in September to Dunhurst, the preparatory school for Bedales where my Uncle Hector was headmaster. However, before then we all went back to Uganda. John had to go unexpectedly three weeks early as Bill Marquand, his assistant had been taken ill. That left me to pack up Copper Beeches; dragging heavy trunks and boxes gave me a miscarriage at three months. However, this was very competently dealt with at the County Hospital and my mother took Sally and Willy while Daisy Powell at the Forge, who most faithfully helped us all for 15 years at Copper Beeches, took care of Catherine and Peter. I emerged, rather feeble, after 48 hours to coincide with a strike of BOAC pilots. Somehow or other we were all got on to an Alitalia flight to Rome-Athens-Nairobi and after a pretty grim journey we reached Nairobi about 0300 and waited in the dark lounge 'till an Argonaut at about 0800 took us to Entebbe. It was good to be back.

Life at Entebbe continued as before. About this time we got to know James Murray who was our ambassador to the newly independent ex Belgian Rwanda Urundi. He came to stay with us several times and was an interesting new acquaintance, coming from a different world to the Colonial one we knew. He was stimulating company and it was as a result of getting to know him that I was prompted to start reading again, history, philosophy and later art and literature, which helped to fill the void left by leaving Uganda.

Sally went back in September and John's parents, who were by now living in Langton Green as his father had had to leave Chilham after a heart attack, looked after her and took her down to Dunhurst. David had gone to Shrewsbury in the summer leaving Lawrence alone at St. Bedes. All three children came out for the Christmas holidays and we went with the four older ones to the game part at the Murchison Falls, chiefly memorable for seeing an elephant taking the washing off a line in the hotel camp grounds. On the way there we spent a night in rather a seedy hotel at Masindi

David, Lawrence, Olive, Sally and William
at Murchison Falls

which had been the Provincial Headquarters of the Western Province before Fort Portal. During the '30s Uganda had become very prosperous with the sale of cotton and coffee and some large and handsome houses had been built in several of the stations. Masindi had some particularly good ones and so had Mbale. The golf course at Masindi was still maintained when we were there and in the evening I wandered around looking at the houses, already by then occupied by Africans, lots of children, goats and chickens where previous memsahibs had had their gardens and I had a pleasurable sensation of 'Sic transit gloria mundi.'

Meanwhile political affairs developed in their own way. Sir Walter Coutts (Wally, Pip Coutts' elder brother) succeeded Freddy Crawford and Duncan Sandys managed to get the various parties to accept a constitution for Independence in October 1962 which meant that we would be able to get away satisfactorily whatever happened afterwards. There were more elections which the UPC won and Obote became Chief Minister and John became Secretary to the Ministry of Internal Affairs working for a large Musoga called Nadiope with whom he had some fairly hairy plane journeys.

Richard was born on June 14 1962, our seventh child and last, after all as Aunt Bo wrote to John seven is a lucky number. When he was 6 weeks old we went back to England for 6 weeks leave. He had been a good, easy baby until then, so it was an unwelcome surprise when, as soon as I carried him into the 'plane, he started to scream and continued screaming, except when being fed, until we reached London. Then he slept for 12 hours; but we cannot have been welcome fellow travellers for the other passengers.

We then had six weeks at Copper Beeches with walks on the Black Mountains and in Radnorshire, and also the celebration of my 40th birthday with a tea party at Farmore and a cake with 40 candles stuck all over and round the sides. As every woman probably feels, 40 is a very climactic birthday and I felt solemn and rather sombre as it approached; but once it was over I realised with pleasure that I felt no different, so what had all the worry been about? We had a few days in London in September when I bought myself a dress in Harrods for the Independence Ball and when Catherine, aged six, distinguished herself by showing the assistant that she knew that 40 + 10 = 50. While the girl had been trying to persuade me to buy a particular dress she had said: (they did talk like that still in the early 60's) "And this one, Madam, will still be fashionable in 10 years time". Catherine's eyes flickered and she took it up at once: "In 10 years time, Mummy, you'll be 50!" Just what I needed to encourage my morale. We left London by plane on a stormy September evening and were back in Uganda next day. Richard gave no trouble that time.

23. October 1962 — June 1963
Uganda: Independence & Farewell

By October 1962 so many colonial territories had become independent that a formula for the Independence handover and celebrations had developed with adjustments for particular circumstances. Richard Posnett was in charge of the proceedings in Uganda. I cannot remember all the details but I think that RAF Middle East, then centred in Aden, provided the service presence and a band which later toured the various district H.Q's and was greatly admireed. Air Vice Marshall Fred Rosier and his wife, Hetty, came over in charge and stayed with us. They were very good company and Catherine flirted shamelessly with Fred, much to Hetty's amusement. Air Marshall Sir Charles Ellworthy was in overall command and John had a game of golf with him. There was a party for the RAF at the Entebbe club at which all the most attractive Entebbe ladies put out their charms, unfortunately there was disillusionment all round, the youngest of the women was into her 30s while none of the young men were over 24 and their disappointment was obvious. I danced with a mature Scottish sergeant who thought it all a great joke.

The Duke and Duchess of Kent came out to represent the crown and stayed at Government House with the Coutts, Wally Coutts was to become Governor General for a short while afterwards. The Kents were generally liked but some of their staff were demanding and troublesome. The hand over ceremony took place in the Kampala stadium preceded by tribal dancing, military parades and speeches. Jomo Kenyatta, who had recently been released from internment, was there and got a good reception from the Africans — he behaved very well. Everyone was very good humoured. At

105

midnight the Uganda flag was raised and the Union Jack lowered and that was that and we went home to 49 Circular Rd and found Jeneti and Kiiza on guard with golf clubs in case there should be any trouble, but there wasn't any at any time. The following day the Independence Ball took place, again in Kampala though I can't remember where. However, I wore my Harrods dress for the first, and last time. The Obotes danced with the Duke and Duchess very well, and then we all joined in, things became increasingly relaxed but never got out of hand. We were sitting with the Russian ambassador to Somaliland who had good English and was amusing and likeable. He had a "Minder" with him a pale, flabby young man who hardly spoke. I would have liked to dance with the ambassador; but instead had to put up with the "Minder", horrible and a bit creepy. A Conservative M.P., Bernard Braine, who was very drunk, came to our table and tried to score off the ambassador; but honours went the other way. I also danced with Felix Rwambarali, one of the radical local politicians whom I rather liked. When, using a bit of 'ta'arof, (ask an Iranian what that means) I said "Let me congratulate you on achieving your Independence", he shamed me by spontaneous delight, "You are most generous", and nearly danced me off my feet. I think that in Amin's time he came to a nasty end.

One other episode I remember. The Kabaka had several distinctly raffish friends out from the U.K. and elsewhere. Amongst them was a very beautiful young West Indian woman, pale cafe au lait with brilliant eyes and a superb figure. I met her in the Ladies and had to unzip her long satin dress which was too tight for any other procedure, naked underneath she then relieved herself while I waited to do her up again. So much for Independence.

When all the excitement had died down life returned, outwardly, to normal. In fact during our remaining months in Uganda I felt a happier and more relaxed atmosphere with the Africans than at any time before. However, it was obvious that John would have to find another occupation and fortunately he was at just the right age. There is no better time than one's early 40s to take another path, if opportunity offers, and at this time the next direction was clearly visible, because who was going to represent Great Britain in all these new nations? The C.R.O. (Commonwealth Relations Office, soon to be merged with the F.O. and become the F.C.O.) was recruiting new officers, John applied and was accepted for examination and interview early in 1963. The children had come out for the holidays. William was going to St. Bedes and John and they all went back together into the hard, cold winter of '62 – '63. I stayed behind with the three small ones and in due course there came a letter from Lawrence describing walking along the sea front at Eastbourne and ending: "Willy is a human icicle". John was successful in his enterprise and in fact was 1st of the accepted candidates inspite of having succumbed to 'flu while staying with his parents. This was what was know as "Asian Flu", there was a global epidemic at this time and I too caught it, in Uganda. However, we both recovered. During this time my mother came out for a final visit and I remember going with her and the children to visit Kajansi, between Entebbe and Kampala where there was a fish farm surrounded by a eucalyptus plantation and attractive small walks.

The other chldren came out for the Easter holidays for the last time. By then we knew that we were going to leave in June and although I was ready and eager for something new, still there was sadness at the thought of leaving the country and the people that I had grown to like so well. However, we determined to have one final expedition, so we went with all the children to stay in the new Ruwenzori Hotel outside Fort Portal. After nine years it already seemed another country and it was strange to see it again, the same and not the same. However, we drove down once towards Bundibugyo and went for a walk round the crater lake at Saka which we all enjoyed. All the staff came to say "Goodbye" to the children at Entebbe airport on their way back to school. It was at about this time that Jeneti said to me, looking at Richard then 10 months, "Sija kumulaba kutambula", (I shall not see him walk), which was like a knife in my heart and still makes me cry. Jeneti and I wrote to each other twice a year after we left. She seemed all right back with her extended family; but then she wrote of illness and shortly after Amin

Olive, Jeneti, Sally and Peter

took over her letters stopped. We were advised not to make enquiries in case we caused more trouble, so I shall never know whether she just died or whether something more nasty happened. Her brother had been Town Clerk of Kampala and died at about the same time it was said of a heart attack; but it could have been anything. Whatever happened to her she was to me, and my children, a true friend and I think of her always as such.

John was due to start work in the CRO in August, we were leaving Uganda in June so we decided to make the most of the journey home and arranged to go by sea on an Italian ship, the Europa, from Mombasa to Brindisi, taking our car, a Hillman convertible, with us, and drive up through Europe to Le Touquet and fly the car from there to Lydd. This was to take six weeks and we were to have a few days at the Nyali Beach Hotel in Mombassa first. Planning all this was interesting and helped to dispel the sadness at leaving. We sold some of our few possessions, including our double bed to a Goan shopkeeper, I hope it brought him good luck, the rest were packed to go later by sea and early in June the day came. We paid off the staff with bonuses, the car was parked and ready beside the cassia tree we had planted and Craig Donald had come to say Goodbye with champagne. We were all quite cheerful when suddenly Jeneti began to cry, Catherine burst into floods of tears, Peter started up, so we leaped into the car and waving at everyone John drove off and didn't look back. By the time we reached Kampala I felt quite calm and that night at the hotel in Mbale, our first and last place in Uganda, I was looking forward to the future.

24. June — July 1963
Return to England

We drove from Mbale to Nairobi where we spent a night and then put the car on a train which took us all by night down to Mombasa. Kenya had not yet become independent, there were still a few months to go and Geoffrey Ellerton who held the same post there as John had in Uganda came to the train to say 'Goodbye'. At Mombasa we stayed for a few days at the Nyali Beach Hotel, much more comfortable than our last visit to the coast and also much more touristy and commercialised; but pleasant.

In the afternoon of June 13 we boarded the *M.V. Europa* bound for Trieste, as we left the harbour we passed the *Ark Royal* which was there on a courtesy visit. Richard's first birthday was on the following day; but as children under one year on boarding travelled free we were able to take advantage of this concession. And it was a concession because Richard did not like the 'Sala bambini', a cage on the upper deck, provided with toys and a 'Bambinaia', i.e. nursery nanny, where we could leave the children during the mornings. Each morning he sat on the floor holding on to the bars of the cage and screaming. Catherine said after a few days 'Mummy, I think the Bambinaia hates Richard'. It was an excellent arrangement. In the mornings the children were in the Sala bambini while we swam and played games, then we gave the children lunch, before the adults, then they were put to rest, then we ate, then we rested, then we all swam and played, then the children had supper and went to bed, then we drank and had supper and went to bed. And so it went on for about a fortnight in perfect weather, hot and fine. There were several amusing episodes. At Mogadishu, where we lay briefly off shore, people came on board lifted in baskets by a ship's crane, then between Mogadishu and Aden we passed quite close to the *Europa's* sister ship, the *Africa* going the opposite way. On both ships the passengers ran to the side to look and wave, the ships bowed quite steeply to each other. I wondered if the Blue Funnel Line would have approved. We called at Aden and went ashore for a few hours, and Hetty Rosier drove us to the duty free shops in the Crescent where we bought ourselves a short wave portable radio, then a novelty. After Aden we called briefly at a port in Eritrea, I think but cannot be sure, and then proceeded up the Red Sea and through the Suez Canal to the Mediterranean. We were to disembark at Brindisi and two nights before there was a grand, farewell ships dinner and party. Among our fellow passengers were Owen and Rosemary Griffith, also from Uganda, and on that evening we had much Italian champagne together. On deck afterwards they talked of a French drink called Amer Picon which they had enjoyed on their honeymoon. John was wise enough not to be tempted; but I had to try some and as a result was totally knocked out the whole of the next day leaving John to do all the packing and look after the children too. However, all was well at Brindisi and we disembarked into the Hillman and set off for Salerno driving through what is, I think, now Mafia country. I remember the mediaeval hill top villages and otherwise empty, natural countryside.

We spent three nights at Salerno in a not very attractive hotel. On one day we drove round the Sorrento peninsular trying, unsuccessfully, to find where John had been during the war, and on the other we went to see the ruined Greek city of Paestum. It was very hot. There is a photograph of Peter, very red in the face, sitting under an oleander bush with his shoes off. Whenever Peter, not yet four, became fed up he would take his shoes off and sit down, quite alarming in the middle of the main street of Salerno. There was a promenade along the sea front of Salerno with a large, ornamental fountain at one end. As we walked along with Richard in his push chair and Peter, with his shoes on, trotting beside, Catherine ran ahead, plunged her face into this fountain and drank freely. When we got there we saw a large notice saying 'Aqua non Potabile'. We were rather anxious but Catherine was unaffected.

From Salerno we went to Frascati in the hills outside Rome passing through Naples. There were beautiful gardens at Frascati and we walked through them with the children and then sat outside a cafe with chocolate ice creams. All the children, even Catherine, were sun bleached; but Peter was very fair and as he sat licking chocolate a young man came up, lifted his face up and said, if I remember right, 'Che' bello biondo'! Everywhere in Italy people were extraordinarily kind to the children and we were never made to feel that they were a nuisance. After Frascati we drove north to San Gimignano, avoiding Rome, even then Italian driving techniques were rather surprising to the inexperienced and we preferred the open roads. We spent one night in San Gimignano and in the evening walked the walls and admired the towers and the splendid view. On next to Menaggio on Lake Como where we stayed for several days.

Here the hotel, whose name I'm afraid I've forgotten, was a splendid Edwardian building on the lake shore with a pier from which you could swim. It was echoing and superbly old fashioned and, just before the holidays, and in 1963, delightfully empty and relaxing. The food was good and everyone was very friendly. We swam in the lake, Peter looked very sweet in his water wings and he and Richard drew from a fellow guest the flattering comment. 'Regarde les petits enfants, comme ils sont mignons'. I'd never thought of them like that before. We spent one day going a boat trip on the lake and took the children to play in an attractive lake

111

side park. Then it was onwards again and we drove over the San Gothard pass where there was still some dirty snow lying, into Switzerland and to Bassersdorf near Zurich where my brother David, who was studying Jungian analysis, was staying with his family. We spent a few days there, visiting the Rheinfall on one of them, and then drove on into France crossing the border near Pontarlier and spending a night in Salins les Bains in a very old fashioned hotel, no ensuite bathrooms then; but a very remote, dark, oaken privy up some steep stairs. Again we walked in the park and then drove on the next day to Gien and from there to Bayeux where we saw the tapestry and cathedral. And, finally, to Le Touquet for one night and the following day, by air, Hillman and all, to Lydd in Kent. Here there was a slight confusion with the customs because when they enquired about the short wave radio we attempted to pass it off casually as quite a long time possession.

Catherine was having none of this and spoke out: 'But Mummy you know you bought that in Aden'. I trod on her toe. 'Oh, Mummy why have you done that to me?' The customs officer was most skilful, he let us have the radio free; but made us pay full duty on all the wine we had bought in France. After Lydd we went to stay with my brother Stopford at Lightlands and from there to Copper Beeches. This whole journey was in every way a fine ending to our 17 years in Uganda.

25. 1963 – 1968
London and Copper Beeches

John was due to start work in the CRO, as it was then, in late August so somewhere had to be found to live in London. John had taken part of his Uganda pension in a lump sum and my mother also helped so money was available and after a day in London looking at flats he settled on Flat 3, 1 Redington Gardens, N.W.3 almost certainly due to the personality of the attractive test pilot's wife who was offering it completely furnished for £10,000. Sally later sold it in the '80s for £42,000.

It was the top flat in a handsome 3 story house at the end of a cul de sac, quiet and near the Heath and with an old fashioned private school, Heysham House, just behind it where Catherine went for three years, and Peter for a short time later. The only disadvantage was the occupant of the flat beneath us, a 'Gay' oldish Inspector of Schools who found the merry stamp of children's feet running above him not to his taste and complained a lot. However, when silence fell in the holidays as we went down to Copper Beeches he became reconciled to us; but never friendly.

After a holiday in Copper Beeches I went up to join John in London for the next term and so a pattern developed which was to last all the time John was working in London, term times in town with weekends in Copper Beeches, and then, for me, the school holidays down in the country with John coming down at weekends. From being a senior official in Uganda John found himself at 42 a Principal in the CRO; but he was always treated tactfully and with consideration and our only complaint was the petty, bureaucratic meanness whereby he was only allowed five weeks holiday a year despite having served HMG already for 17 years.

Rather to my surprise I found I enjoyed living in London. The children seemed to accept the restricted way of life although I had trouble persuading Peter not to run into people's gardens to pee and not to run straight across roads. After one particularly alarming dash over Frognal I reckoned that if he surived a month all would be well and so it turned out. John would leave for work, which started at 1000 and went on till 1800, at about 0900 taking school goers with him, though at Heysham they could walk through adjoining gardens. I would clear up and do shopping, washing and other domestic chores. In the afternoons I would go with Peter and Richard to Golders Hill Park. Mary Sibley who 'did' for our gay neighbour, also came to 'do' for us and to baby sit. This was wonderful. Once a week I would have a day off and go into town to look at art galleries and exhibitions and also to spend money at Harrods. I was only allowed to do this once a term! In the evenings we went to concerts, theatres and to the opera and also to play bridge with Henry and Hazel Morris who were living in what was later to become Thatcher land, i.e. North Finchley. Henry became Reader in African Law at the S.O.A.S. We were busy; but not pressurised socially, the children made friends at school and London ways began to be familiar, and there was always the weekly escape to Herefordshire. My mother had stayed on at Farmore after my father's death and was busy making a beautiful garden and was active in a great many local concerns, in fact the final years of her life were fulfilling for her and rewarding, certainly while she was in good health. So there she was, a suitable 'Granny' for the children, not to be taken too lightly but offering lemon sponge cake for tea and television viewing until we acquired our own.

Sometime in the '60s the Foreign Office and the Commonwealth Relations Office were amalgamated to become the FCO. This was a marriage of practical convenience; but not of kindred spirits, the Foreign Office had always recruited 'la Creme de la creme' socially and intellectually, or so they thought, while the CRO were a pretty average lot of standard civil servants. To give an example of what I mean: there was a CRO wives' organisation called, not surprisingly, the CROWS. I went to one, and one only, meeting in the India Office library. There a senior CROW lady, complete with pearls, gave a talk to a large cluster of lesser CROWS on the importance of learning how to enter big rooms! However, John benefited greatly from the enlarged opportunities and very soon found himself working in IRD (Information Research Department). This was a sort of dirty tricks organisation trying to do down the Russians and their allies by means of propaganda and misleading information, of course the Russians were hard at work doing the same thing so everyone was kept well occupied. It was while working in IRD that he met Rosemary Allott who was later to introduce us to the pleasure and interest of trekking in the Himalaya.

While Peter and Richard were small we took our holidays in Copper Beeches although we did contemplate a visit to northern Scotland one June; but this was aborted by the two little boys getting measles. However, a year or so later we hired a house in Saundersfoot for a fortnight in August and went there with the younger children in the Omnicoach, a large, green Austin van or minibus, which we used for transport round Herefordshire and Wales. It was ideal for family travel, several of the seats in the back were taken out so there was plenty of room for bicycles and baggage, the children could move about and fight if they wanted to and John and I sat, aloof in front, with the youngest between us on the engine, immune from the activities behind, all safely locked in. Saundersfoot was rather seedy; but next year we were introduced by my brother David, to Cerbid near Solva and there we spent several happy holidays. Cerbid was, and still is I believe, a Welsh farmhouse and buildings imaginatively and comfortably converted for holiday letting and we were able to explore Pembrokeshire hills and coast, the boys fished off the rocks for Pollack, we all bathed in the invigorating sea and London seemed another world. We had also acquired a dog, induced to by my mother who knew the breeder, a Welsh corgi called Dylan who travelled around with us from London to Hereford and adapted quite happily to both. It was Catherine's job to take him for his early morning walk before breakfast in London. Mary Sibley, when baby sitting, corrupted him terribly; but he was an attractive little animal.

By 1967 we knew that John would shortly be sent on an overseas posting and we had to consider what to do about the children. Catherine had already gone to Dunhurst. Sally had progressed to Bedales and Peter was to follow the other boys at St. Bedes. He and Richard both went for a while to Northbridge House school in Hampstead where I think they were happy and made friends. Birthday parties in the flat always presented a problem, which we usually solved by having John take a selected party on an outing and bring them all back to tea which I prepared meanwhile. Too much mayhem would not have been acceptable to our neighbours. As it was, our last encounter with one downstairs neighbour,

Mr. Tudhope, was unfortunate. John had gone to Paris on IRD work, the holidays had started, Sally and Catherine were in the flat and we were all going down to Copper Beeches the next day. I put a load of washing into the machine, shut Dylan into the kitchen and sat down to pay bills and write letters. After a while I heard Dylan whimpering; but paid no attention, then there were a few remote thumps — I went into the kitchen and found Dylan in his apple box bed floating in several inches of water. I had forgotten to connect the outflow pipes to the sink. What could be done? We mopped up and waited anxiously for 'Tudders' car to arrive, looking out of the window. It duly did and I heard his flat door open and close. Then there was quite a pause and I was just beginning to think I'd got away with it when the door bell rang, I went to it and there the wretched man stood positively shaking. I went in and alas! his dining room ceiling had come down on top of his polished table, wet plaster was scattered everywhere. At least I wasn't surprised. I assured him we would clear up and make good and he then went out, still shaking. I went up and rang Mary Sibley who, when she could stop laughing, said 'Never mind love, I'll be round' and came and swept it all up and put it in polythene bags which John, next night, put surreptitiously on a skip. She was a good friend. The next day, thankfully, I drove down to Copper Beeches. It cost £46 to repair the ceiling.

In about April 1968 John heard that he was to go to be Head of Chancery in Tehran. So, at last, I was to see Persia. We had one final family holiday in Scotland driving up in two cars, Lawrence, who had recently passed his test, was in charge of one and we had a happy week staying in a hotel at Boat of Garten and visiting sites of Macgregor interest and also seeing for the last time, Cousin Anne who was still living at Nethy Bridge and took us for a slightly unorthodox drive through forest in a Land Rover. Sally and Catherine were wearing the by then, inevitable, blue jeans and Cousin Anne said to me, rather wistfully; "Were you allowed to wear such sensible clothes when you were young?" Well I wasn't; but I think I was better off in that respect than she had been.

Some time in July John left by train to Genoa, by boat to

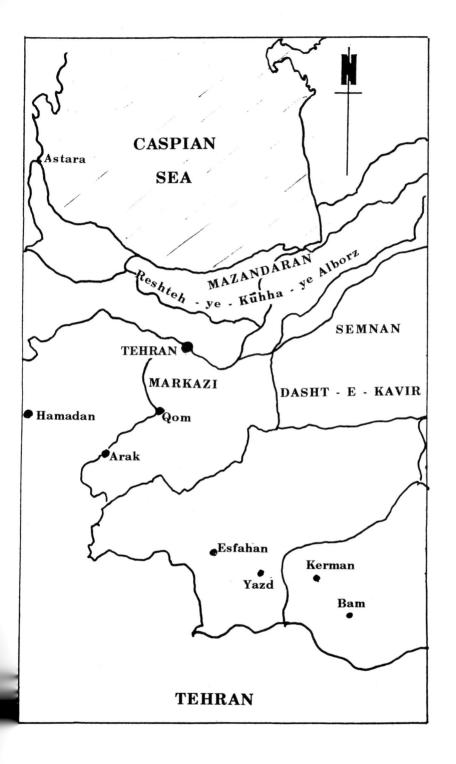

Beirut and thereon by air to Tehran. I went with the family to Cerbid for the summer holidays and then in September left by air to join him. Lawrence had taken his 'A' levels in the summer and left Shrewsbury and was waiting to have an offer from a university to read modern languages. So he came with me and Richard and we had an uneventful flight to Tehran. Back in England Dylan had been found a home in the Golden Valley and arrangements had been made for Catherine's pony, Goldie, to live at stables near Petersfield. So we started, once more, to learn a new way of life.

26. September 1968 — July 1970
Tehran

We arrived at Tehran airport late in the evening and were met by John in a red Triumph Herald that he had bought. The drive from the airport to the embassy was a good introduction to what was to come. Cars, buses, trucks, taxis, bicycles, donkeys, little Japanese vans and people all struggled along in varying directions without any order or system. It was hazardous, noisy, confusing and slow. When we reached the old embassy compound we found that our house, a pleasant, handsome one, originally the consul's, was built along side the Khriaban (Avenue) Firdawsi, one of the main streets. There was usually a pause in the traffic between 0100 and 0430, otherwise the noise was constant and terrific. For the first three nights I couldn't sleep at all, then exhaustion triumphed and I gradually got used to it. Our bedroom looked over the large, well tended embassy gardens with their magnificent plane trees, dating back to 1867 and the ambassador's residence built in Neo Mogul style, but our spare room backed directly on to the street and we always had a small, sadistic pleasure in putting official guests from London to sleep there.

118

Although by 1968 Britain had ceased to have any real power or influence over Middle East affairs the tradition of the past, when we had, still remained. The Anglo Iranian Oil Co. was still important and there were many business and official interests. The embassy was considered important and we were fortunate to have Denis Wright as our ambassador all the time we were there, a fluent speaker of Farsi and with great knowledge of Iran and its people he was also an enthusiastic walker and traveller and introduced us to the pleasures of exploring the hills and valleys of the Elburz mountains which rose dominant to the north of Tehran into the clear, clean air above the normal thick cloud of polluted smog. Social life was intense and strictly graded. The Shah was at his apogee and no doubts troubled his rule, wealth, development, industry, Americans, Japanese, British and French businessmen and officials, scholars and archaeologists all vied with each other together with squalor, urban and rural poverty, and a discontented traditional religion which was eventually to triumph. But when we were there the White Revolution, as the Shah named his policies, seemed established to endure. As Head of Chancery John's contacts were with middle grade government officials, university lecturers and, of course, our fellow diplomats. We made many friends and amongst the best were Zia and Rustum Bayandur, now living in London, whom we still see from time to time.

The main embassy compound in central Tehran was complemented by another at Golhak, higher up the hill where the ambassador had a summer residence and there was also the British Primary School. Here Richard went daily by embassy bus with other embassy children, taking sandwiches with him which usually got eaten on the way. His time in Tehran was one of the few periods in his life when Richard merited the nickname he was given of 'Nibbly Nubbly'. Our household was run by Abbas, the cook, assisted first hy Heydar and then by Ali and with Fatumeh to keep an eye on Richard when we went out in the evening which was very frequent. In fact most evenings we were either entertaining or being entertained. It wasn't so bad in winter; but as I have always woken with the light, summer could be very

On the Elburz above Tehran

exhausting with sleep only from 0100 — 0500 at best and I remember finding myself going to sleep at a Saturday lunch party and only just avoiding disgrace.

Lawrence heard before Christmas that he had a place at Cardiff to read Modern Languages the following autumn and he went back to England after the next holidays. However, while he was with us he did some very pleasant paintings of Iranian scenery and I admired this talent that I totally lack. He also came down with us, and Richard too, to Khorramshahr, later to be distroyed in the Iran — Iraq war, to collect the Land Rover we had bought and which had been sent out by sea. We went down by train. Richard was very curious about the very primitive latrine. We spent a night with the British Council at Khorramshahr and drove back by Ahwaz and Hamadan, visiting the great dam at Dezful on the way.

John was kept hard at it in the office; but I had plenty of

time free and, encouraged by Maria Wiggin, started riding at a stables up beyond Tajrish run by Colonel and Mrs. Shaki. This was very different from riding Lily or even GPB. All the horses were stallions and the technique of riding them involved leaning hard on the heavy curb bit and just staying on while they galloped, barely in control, over desert and dry wadis. At first I was fairly scared; but once I found I could do it I thoroughly enjoyed it. Usually Colonel Shaki came out with us and things were well disciplined; but sometimes his wife, a red headed German who rode a huge white stallion, would take charge and this was terrifying as she was ruthless and, I suspect, was trying to avenge the last war. The Shakis lived in separate houses and never spoke to each other except about horses which bound them together. When they decided I was fairly reliable I was allowed to go out on my own and Catherine in the holidays came too. Once we were set upon by a pack of wild dogs and one got Catherine's horse by the tail; but he kicked himself free. Packs of these dogs roamed the waste land around Tehran and on one occasion killed a shepherd boy. After this poisoned meat was scattered freely and for some time afterwards our rides were enlivened by the stench of rotting dog.

The other activity, apart from walking the wonderful mountains of the Elburz which was a spring and summer recreation, was skiing which we could do at Ab Ali, about an hours drive to the east. We used to go there on Sundays, taking a picnic and some madeira. We would ski all morning till tired, come back to the Land Rover, have our soup, half a bottle of Madeira and then drive back to Tehran, fighting off sleep. The children all learned to ski there and Richard became quite dashing; but never leaned to turn, he would go up to the top of the ski lift and then zoom down scattering the learners on his way. Once he came proudly to us and said "I've just knocked down 11 Americans!"

The children at school in England were by now allowed two free air passages a year to join us — on the third holiday I would go back to Copper Beeches — the London flat was let — which was occupied by David and Lawrence, both of them at university. The summer in Tehran was hot and disagreeable so I chose that time for my England holiday, leaving John to sweat it out on his own. John was allowed two weeks local leave each year during his time in Iran and each Spring holidays he would take this leave and we would go off with the children in the Land Rover and make some long and interesting expeditions. Term times at the Tehran primary school were different from those in England so Richard found himself staying with the Breezes when we went on these expeditions and felt hard done by. But he was able to come with us on many short weekend trips when the others were at school so I don't think he had much real cause for complaint. On one of these excursions we went to spend a couple of nights by the Caspian in a hotel by the lake, very different country from what we were used to, green with rice fields, gardens and woods, it must have been May because I remember hearing the cuckoo, a strangely nostalgic sound in the mild, moist air. Pools full of frogs were very interesting to Richard and early one morning he came to wake us: "Come quickly I've just seen a frog eaten by a snake!". Terrapins were also plentiful; but unfortunately they would try to cross the main road which was dotted with their crushed carcases.

27. Travels in Iran 1969 — 1970

As I have said, we took advantage of the U.K. school Easter holidays to benefit from John's allowance of local leave and made two long excursions. The Shah's government was trying to develope the tourist trade and so hotels were available in the main attractive sites — these provided basic western style facilities though some of the ablution and toilet arrangements were rather unconventional. However, females were accepted as quests on the same terms as males — in other less tourist frequented parts there were problems and we usually found ourselves eating in our bedroom, everybody would be very polite; but I was definitely not welcome in the public dining area.

No such problems occurred on our first journey in April 1969 which was to Isfahan and Shiraz, both prime tourist sites. We set off with Sally, William, Catherine and Peter in the long wheel based Land Rover and drove in a day down to Isfahan where we spent two nights. On the way down while turning a corner on a mountain road we suddenly came upon what looked like about a hundred yards of rather bumpy dirty felt on the road. I suddenly realised that it was the remains of a flock of sheep run over by one truck and then rolled over and flattened by others. It was rather surprising; but later in Jordan we saw signs of a similar event only with a couple of donkeys instead of sheep. After all they were dead and useless so why bother to remove them?

In Isfahan we visited the madrasseh, mosques and bridges. I will not bother to describe them, the best guide to what they were like at that time is the book by Denis Wright, James Morris (as he was then) and Roger Wood. I believe they were damaged during the Iran — Iraq war, if so it only shows the futility of human endeavours; but I remember the dome of the Lutfullah mosque with its exquisite tiling reaching towards infinity and the whole building filled with a feeling of awe, the most spiritual of all the mosques that I have seen.

From Isfahan we went on to Shiraz stopping at Pasargardae and Persepolis on the way. I am glad to have seen Persepolis but its interest for me was historical and archaeological, whereas the tomb of Cyrus, alone in its grove of trees and with the remains of the palace close at hand again had a more than merely academic significance. We visited Nagsh-e-Rustam as well and saw the relief of the defeated Roman emperors, Philip and Valerian cowering before their Sassanian conqueror.

Shiraz was pleasant, the hotel was comfortable, it was fine and warm but not yet hot and the roses were in full flower in all the well kept public gardens. We saw the tombs of Sa'adi and Hafez and drove south towards the land of the Qashqai to see Qaleh-e-Dokhtar, a ruined Sassanian castle of about AD200 perched on a crag above a river. We all scrambled up and explored and there again we heard the cuckoo.

The following winter David, who was at Balliol reading physics, came out as well as the other children and we made a cold, grey journey to the north west to Zanjan and into the open country to Sultaniyeh to see the tomb of Oljeitu one of the Mongol kings. This was very ruined; but still had remains of fine blue tiling. No one else was there and in the wind and light dusting of snow with a small, dingy village below where we had tea later I thought of Ozymandias King of Kings. While we were having tea we talked with the friendly villagers, by now John and I could get by in simple Farsi, and he asked them what they did to earn a living, "Hichi, faqut keshavarzi" — Nothing there is only farming! From such villages all over Asia the young men go to the vast cities and join the swarming urban poor. Myself I think I should prefer to stay where I was; but everyone has always thought the streets of cities are paved with gold, and so they are; but only a few get to walk on the gold paving.

The following April we made our most ambitious journey. This time Lawrence was with us too and very fortunately as he was most helpful with wheel changing. We set off to cross the desert to Yazd. As we drove through the slums of south Tehran I realised, with a sinking heart, that I had forgotten to bring the necessary bottle of whisky. I knew that it would be most unwise to mention this while John was negotiating the hazards of Tehran traffic so later, as we went through the desert, I said that I thought it would probably be good for us to abstain for a while. This was not very well received; but fortunately in all the places we stayed there was good local wine to be found. The hotel at Yazd was comfortable and we found a good guide who took us to the mosque. The two girls and I were given chadors (black cloaks) to wear. I rather liked them — you could hide from curious locals, and as Sally will remember, foreign females in their indecent and ridiculous clothing, could provoke a lot of teasing from the locals. We also visited the Zoroastrian tower of silence and drove up into a side valley where there was an old walled town surrounded by gardens.

The following day we drove on to Kerman and on the way had our first puncture. It was lucky that Lawrence was able to help as jacking the Land Rover on a slope was hard work.

The hotel at Kerman was pretty scruffy; but had an attractive garden. We were adopted by a young student called Mansur who took us to the bazaar, to a carpet factory and to the hamam (baths) which we might not otherwise have seen. Rather to our surprise he refused any payment so later we sent him a book. The following day we went first to Mahan where the tomb of Shah Nematullah is one of the most beautiful in Iran, and then across the mountain and desert to Bam. The old city of Bam ran out of water in the 19th century and was abandoned. It remains untouched except by time and we spent the afternoon exploring it and climbed up to the citadel from which we could see Peter, who had got left behind, as he often did, running along the dusty lanes looking for us. We found him all right afterwards. On the way back to Kerman there was another puncture. The previous one had been patched in Kerman but not very well and so we were left with a drive back with no spare wheel on an April evening over barren, empty hills and along a rough road with neither food nor warm clothing. It was anxious. We all sat in complete silence while John drove with great care and at a slow speed. The sound of the wheels on tarmac shortly after Mahan was pleasant music. The next day we bought a new tyre and got back to Tehran without further trouble.

John and I made a weekend journey to the eastern Caspian with Richard to see the great tomb tower of Gonbad-e-Qabus. Shams al Ma'ali Qabus ruled in the area between 976 — 1012 A.D. His tomb is one of the renowned wonders of Iran — it was a pity that when we saw it was clothed in scaffolding. On the way there we stopped by the shores of the Caspian; but it was June and the sand was so hot that Richard could hardly bear to cross it to reach the water so we didn't stay long. The hotel where we stayed was having no nonsense with foreign females and we all ate in our room. I was kept awake most of the night by barking dogs and the drive back the next day was long and very tiring, over 12 hours; but Richard never complained, and anyway I have seen the Gonbad-e-Qabus.

We made many other weekend trips, sometimes camping in the mountains in summer, we had a little, portable gas cooker on which we could heat soup and boil eggs and make tea and coffee, so we were able to be self sufficient for a short time. Richard came with us on all these occasions until he went to St. Bedes.

Our last journey was to Sanandaj and Kermanshah. There was a Christian hospital in a Kurdish town, I'm afraid I can't remember its name, which was asking for official U.K. support and John was sent to assess the situation. We were taken around by the dedicated doctor in charge and given a meal by him and his equally self sacrificing wife. But alas, a Christian hospital with crucifixes over the beds, did not have much chance in Sunni Kurdistan and in this quite large hospital, built, I think, with Canadian money, we only saw one patient, so I'm afraid John was not able to recommend an injection of U.K. taxpayer's money.

This reminds me of a sidelight I was given on Overseas Aid. In summer 1970 we had a visit from the head ODA official in charge of the Middle East. Why the oil rich Middle East needed Aid is irrelevant. The first secretary in charge of Aid gave a party for this man, rather a jolly character. He was telling me a funny story about a cotton ginnery provided for Tabriz by the British taxpayer. For those who don't know, the seeds in cotton have to be removed before it can be spun and this process is called 'ginning' and a factory that does it is called a ginnery. Well unfortunately the machines in this ginnery, which had cost the British taxpayers about £2,000,000, were the wrong size for Iranian cotton and so were quietly rusting away. After he had told me this with much laughter, I asked "Well about how much British Aid does get wasted?" "Oh", he said, helping himself to another whisky, "about 60%; but never mind it gives me and a lot of other people a jolly good way of life." And why not?

To continue on our journey to Sanandaj — we left the hospital in the afternoon and drove down off the plateau into a valley arriving at Sanandaj at dusk. Here we had our passports carefully scrutinised by Savak (the secret police) and were allowed to stay in rather a scruffy hotel, no question of me being allowed into the main area and we had our meal in our chilly bedroom. There was a particularly unsavoury latrine up some steps at the end of the passage.

The following day we drove down through Luristan to Kermanshah and from there to Hamadan where we spent the night in a more western style hotel. At Kermanshah we stopped long enough to look at the monument to Darius and Bisitun and the Sassanian carvings at Taq'e Bustan. I cannot remember which of these sites has also got engraved on a slab in large English capitals the name of someone who must have been there when Henry Rawlinson was at work deciphering the inscriptions in the 1840s.

28. July 1970 — January 1971
Tehran — England — Tehran — Jordan

In July 1970 I went back to England for the summer holidays and John followed later on leave. Richard went to St. Bedes in September and afterwards we had our first holiday without children since 1949. We went to Mull for two weeks and stayed at a hotel in Tobermory. We visited Iona of which John had childhood memories, and did a great deal of walking, including going up Ben More in pouring rain. However, we ate and drank so well in the hotel that despite all the walking we each put on a pound a day in weight which was rather disconcerting. When we got back to Copper Beeches John was rung up one day by Personnel from the FCO with the news that he had been appointed Counsellor/ Head of Chancery in Amman and was to go at the end of January. The Black September rising when the Palestinians tried to throw out the Hashemites had only just been put down, so when John hesitated on the phone he was thought to be reluctant to go; but not so, he next said, "It will be like going home", and so indeed it was as he had spent several boyhood holidays there when his father was in what was then TransJordan as adviser to the Emir Abdallah. So when we went back to Tehran at the end of October it was for the last time. The children came out for Christmas and we had the usual skiing expeditions. We also attempted some cross country skiing which I rather enjoyed and regret not having been able to do more, the terrain was kinder than it had been at Lenzerheide.

On January 29th, we set off from Tehran in our Land Rover taking our basic belongings with us. The rest followed later by lorry. The Wrights had given us a good farewell dinner party at which nice things were said about us both and John said nice things about everybody else. I was sorry to leave; but as always interested and stimulated by the thought of something new. The weather was grey and chilly; but not bad and we made Kermanshah for the first night without problem. We stayed in a large, cold, empty hotel with no feeding arrangements so we had to go to a cafe where I was just tolerated. We were put far away at the back and were only allowed one course; but it was enough and we went back to our damp beds and slept well. The next day we drove over grey and gloomy hills covered with a sprinkling of dirty snow and crossed the border into Iraq at Qasr-e-Shirin. There were no problems. We drove on towards Baghdad stopping in some grubby hills to boil up some soup. On both sides of the border there were a number of army camps. Western military attaches, when considering the armed potential of Iran and Iraq, always said, when we were there, that if they went to war the only question would be who ran away first. Later, eight years of inconclusive, but savage and unyielding, fighting proved how wrong they were. On the other hand the Gulf war showed quite clearly the overwhelming superiority of Western technology, efficiently applied.

We spent a night in Baghdad staying with a hospitable, friendly FCO colleague. The little I saw of Baghdad did not make me want to stay longer. The next day we set off across the desert for Jordan. The weather was cloudy; but quite mild and the drive was uneventful, the road was narrow but well surfaced and with care we could pass and be passed by heavy lorries without having to give way. At midday we drove off the road behind a little ridge and had our soup and rest, it was possible to imagine the road and the lorries did not exist. We crossed the border at the Iraq control and carried on along the route of a disused pipe line to H4 which had been, as its name denotes an oil pumping station. Here there was a chilly rest house but we were able to have a meal and a shower and a bed and felt pleased to have got so far. Crossing the Jordanian border control the next day was interesting as John's diplomatic passport showed that he had been born in Hebron, Palestine, now part of the Israeli-occupied territories; but then, in 1921 before the post 1914 – 18 war peace treaties had been signed, still part of the defunct Ottoman Empire. However, after a certain amount of interest we were allowed through and duly arrived in Amman about dusk.

The Land Rover performed admirably. However, we faced a problem with it in Jordan. Land Rovers were boycotted as part of the Arab boycott of all businesses or organisations which had dealing with Israel. We had driven across with our Tehran diplomatic number plates; but these had to be sent back and we should never be able to get any Jordanian ones. However, a simple solution, acceptable to all was found. the Tehran plates were duly sent back and John carefully painted duplicates which he attached to the Land Rover which remained with us all the time we were in Jordan and was eventually sold to the father of King Hussein's then Queen.

Although the September rising had been effectively crushed by the Jordanian army there was still occasional spasmodic firing at night and life had not yet returned to normal. Our house was above the 3rd circle and the embassy buildings, in a pleasant tree lined road with other diplomatic houses all around. Higher up was the ambassador's house, the embassy club with pool and tennis court and beyond that a new hotel with large swimming pool. Then there was open country. Diplomatic social life had by no means got going again and it was pleasant to have quiet evenings in our still sandbagged house and restful after the social whirl of Tehran. So when veterans of the September conflict asked me how I found Amman and I said it seemed blissfully quiet, I got the impression that I had somehow said the wrong thing.

129

29. January 1971 — March 1973
Jordan

We arrived in Jordan at a very favourable time. The Hashemites had indisputably put down the Palestinians and although during our first few months there were occasional skirmishes there was no longer any serious threat to stability. At the same time tourism and all its attendant drawbacks had not got going again. Nor had the great urban development which surged following the conflicts in Lebanon and again, I understand, after the expulsion of Palestinians from Kuwait following the Gulf war. So although there were the standard, modern, ugly concrete block buildings rearing up on the hills much remained of the old town and we would walk down from our house to the first circle and then past the house which John remembered as his parents' during holidays in the 30's. Also the many ancient and beautiful sites from Roman, Arabic and Crusader times were uncrowded and indeed, usually solitary. And the beach at Aqaba had no high rise hotels, only bungalow type hostelries and the beach itself was almost empty though you did have to beware, while swimming of sewage from ships at anchor in the bay.

Politically the situation was interesting. Although the Hashemites were seemingly secure there was a very large, in fact, I think, a majority Palestinian population, many of them expelled from the West Bank after the 1967 Israeli invasion. So the government was continually and necessarily on the alert against terrorism and intrigue. While we were there the Prime Minister Wasfi'Tel was assassinated in Egypt. John's predecessor had been removed because he became too friendly with Palestinians and in 1972 a similar fate befell John Phillips who was ambassador when we arrived.

After John Phillips left there was a period of several months when John was Chargé and then Glen Balfour Paul arrived. His wife had died recently and he was left with four children. Subsequently he remarried and we went to his wedding which I shall tell of in due course. From my point of view it meant that as the senior British lady (!) I had all the chores with none of the status of an ambassador's wife. I had to sit on fund raising committees for various charities including Save the Children and had to do whatever everybody else wanted. There was a pleasant dentist called Afif Kafeena, married to a Scotswoman, who had theatrical ambitions and proposed to put on a fund raising performance in aid of the SCF. First he suggested Julius Caesar, then Macbeth but both were discouraged for political reasons. Finally, he settled for Pygmalion. After a great deal of work this was staged in the Roman amphitheatre at Jerash in late August 1972, no expense was spared including packed supper dishes. When it was all over and the accounts were being given to the managing committee the results were read out: Expenditure 2,000 Dinars, Takings 2,028 Dinars. After a slight pause we were all most effusive in our thanks and hurried on to the next business. Afif Kafeena later had the stuggle of extracting, under local anaesthetic, two impacted wisdom teeth from Sally who refused to have a general anaesthetic. It took 1½ hours and I do not think Sally would wish to repeat the performance!

While we were in Jordan the children who were still at school came out for every holiday and at the end of the summer one I would go back for a few weeks to see that all was well. David and Lawrence were living in Copper Beeches at the time, Daisy Powell heroically looked after the house. On the way down from London in the train I used to say to myself "Whatever it's like I'm not going to lose my temper". Fortunately they only occupied two rooms and I found that 24 hours hard work made the place habitable again. After Pygmalion the flight back to England was unusually trying. Jordanian airlines, Alia, ran a cut price flight between Tehran — London overflying Egypt, Lebanon even then being considered unreliable. We, that is myself, Catherine, Peter and Richard boarded about midday expecting a five hour flight. While starting the engines the power failed. We sat there in a crowded aircraft in the heat with no air conditioning for about 15 minutes — it seemed much longer — and were then let off before anybody died. After about an hour we boarded again and set off for Frankfurt. We had unexpected travelling comnpanions in Richard and Sarah Wood, Richard had been a friend in Tehran, who were on their way home by Alia. At Frankfurt we disembarked for refuelling and then took off into a massive thunderstorm — the plane shook and fell, crockery crashed, lightning flashed and I was terrified, so was Richard Wood who was sitting next to me. Not so Sarah on the other side of the aisle — she looked at her husband's and my faces and said, "I think whisky is called for" and filled an aircraft beaker with duty free whisky which restored us both wonderfully and I remember looking out with glory at the massive clouds, the violent lightning and finally the mysterious moon. I think it was on the return journey that I spent a night in Beirut with Peter and Rosie Joy in their beautiful, traditional house in the old town by the sea. I wonder what has happened to it now.

The Land Rover enabled us to visit almost all the ancient and well known historical sites and monuments and many of the less well known ones. In spite of all the trouble and of our political feebleness the British were surprisingly well liked in Jordan, police and soldiers waved us through check points disregarding our unconventional number plates and local people responded gladly to our attempts at Arabic speaking. We never even reached the standard we had in Farsi — perhaps we were getting too old.

As I am not trying to write a guide book I will not tell of too many sites; but must especially mention Petra which we visited many times and there became good friends with Haroun, one of the guides, who took us to several remote tombs and also up to the summit of Umm al Byara, quite a hard climb. And at the end of our time in Jordan John, I and Sally were allowed to go up Jebel Haroun among the first foreigners to do so (Sally and I were definitely the first females). We were taken up on horse back. Sally's horse had suicidal tendencies so I took it over on the way down. I should have preferred to walk. At the summit there was a flat, grassy area — the tomb itself is built into the rock, you enter it by descending steps, there are two chambers within, the farthest contains the tomb behind a curtain. Sally and I were not sure if we would be allowed in so we stayed outside; but were called to come and felt it a great privilege. I do not know who is in fact buried there almost certainly not Aaron;; but the atmosphere spoke of something holy though architecturally the tomb is not impressive. We drove through the Wadi Rumm several times on our way to Aqaba and once spent a night there. There was barely a track and no other people. Lawrence who was out on holiday slept on top of the Land Rover, the other children inside it and John and I on camp beds outside. I did not sleep very well from thinking of scorpions. One of our last visits was to Umm al Jamal, a Nabataean town of basalt in ruins towards the eastern border of Jordan. John, I and Sally went with Glen Balfour Paul, some of his family and his guard dog Druid, a magnificent Alsatian, whom I would not have wanted to annoy. The herding instinct was strong in Druid and whenever we strayed too far from the main group he would round us up, politely but firmly. He also was very suspicious of Arabs which caused some embarrassment when senior Jordanian government officials called on the British ambassador.

While we were there Crystal Bennett was head of the British School of Archaeology in Amman. We got to know her well and were taken by her to see several interesting 'digs' including one at Bosra and another at Buseirah. Richard became very enthusiastic and later in 1980 between school and university where, needless to say, he read Archaeology, he went out for several months to Jordan again and took part in a number of 'digs'.

Early in 1973 John was appointed Assistant Secretary for the remaining Dependent Territories in the FCO and on March 14 Sally and I left by air for England. I went 1st class and enjoyed myself with free drinks and an amusing ex-security policeman whose name I forget. Sally was crushed between two Arabs in Economy and could see with envious disapproval that I was having a good time. But perhaps her feelings were influenced by the fact that the night before, on her birthday, while John and I were attending an immense farewell party given for us by rather a nice Jordanian doctor, who had succeeded in curing John of a plague of boils which had defeated the British medical establishment, she had been given a generous amount of good claret by Bill Speares! John himself had a slow and very uncomfortable flight back in an RAF plane accompanying home a visiting British Minister.

30. April 1973 — November 1975
England and journey to New Hebrides

Once back in England life settled into the same pattern as in 1963 – 68 but with the difference that all the children were either at school, college or at work. David, who had left Balliol in 1971 and then gone to Manchester to take an Msc was working in London for GEC and living in the Redington Gardens flat, Sally, soon after we returned found work as a P.A. to one of the directors of the Covent Garden Opera House, Lawrence was starting work for the Revenue, William was at Shrewsbury, Catherine at Bedales, Peter and Richard still at St. Bedes. So once John, David and Sally had left for work I had the day to myself and spent it happily in mild domestic chores, visits to art exhibitions and museums and, of course, the occasional trip to Harrods. Without any moral effort I reduced myself to a size 12 (not for long), after all there was no need to cook a large midday meal and all John wanted after business lunches was soup in the evening, and whisky, of course. We went to concerts and theatres and often to the Opera where Sally was able to get us good seats at reasonable prices. In the holidays and at weekends we went down to Copper Beeches and in August John would take leave and come down to Cerbid where we swam and explored the beaches of Pembrokeshire and also the Prescelly mountains.

John settled happily into the FCO again and brought home some funny stories of curious goings on in the odd dependent territories, particularly I seem to remember in Tristan da Cunha. In July 1973 I went with him on an official visit to Gibraltar where Varyl Begg was Governor with his friendly wife Rosemany. We stayed a few nights in Government House, a large, echoing relic of distant glories with a great, high, dark ballroom adorned with huge, long portraits of past royalty. I was particularly impressed by the one of Queen Alexandra. There was also a room said to be haunted, which no one would ever sleep in and containing only an ancient truckle bed, and there was, too, a private peep hole into the adjoining chapel. A new, modest wing housed the present establishment. A dinner party was given for us and towards the end the keys to the fortress were ceremoniously brought in by a sergeant and placed beside the Governor. We climbed up to the top of the Rock, saw the caves and some old gun emplacements and I remember also visiting a cemetery and reading the stones commemorating vanished soldiers and sailors now absorbed into the distant past.

1973 was also notable for the Yom Kippur war when the Egyptians very nearly beat the Israelis but were unable to follow up and so failed. This provoked an Arab oil embargo and closure of the Suez canal which gave the rich Western economies a nasty shock but the Arab oil producers were not prepared to see it through and so the wretched Arab/Israeli confrontation drags on to this day. I would be prepared to bet that it will continue longer than I do — neither side has the necessary magnanimity. At the same time as the oil embargo there occurred the first miners' strike, the one that Arthur Scargill won. I could never understand how Ted Heath could be so stupid as not to realise that the oil embargo offerred him a face-saving way out. But he didn't and when in March 1974 he went to the country he was very properly thrown out and we had Harold Wilson to lead us again. I rather admired Harold Wilson for one thing and that was the way he could adapt his voice to the circumstances. He had three special tones: 1) When addressing trade unionists it was "Ah'm joost a working class lad like all of you": 2) Talking on slightly intellectual subjects he was the

135

clever Oxford graduate, and 3) on television there was a vibrant cosy note, "I am the Father of my people".

At Copper Beeches during the holidays I started riding with Catherine. We bought for her a handsome grey gelding called Talisman and Catherine and I, on Goldie, had many happy rides through Aconbury woods and over the fields beyond Dewsall. We acquired a horse box and in the autumn and winter of 1974 by which time Catherine was 18, she would go out with the South Hereford hunt and John and I followed on foot. It was decided to get Goldie in foal and here I know I made a mistake. The experts advised a sensible Welsh cob; but I wanted something more exciting and so Goldie was taken to Cusop Guardsman, a little thoroughbred and in May 1975 Ahu was born, a beautiful little bay filly; but alas, very temperamental. All the experts shook their heads and said "I told you so" and they were right. We had a Persian, Azer Amirali staying with us at the time and it was she who gave Ahu her name, the Persian for gazelle.

At the end of August 1974 Lawrence and Heather Brown were married in Bath. William Morris had also married shortly before and we went through a stage of going to the weddings of friends' children. Lawrence had been subjected to a fairly fierce pre-wedding party by his friends and I was impressed by how well he managed to carry out all his necessary bridegroom duties. They made a very handsome and attractive pair.

In the autumn of 1974 we went to Glen Balfour Paul's wedding. His bride came from Devon and the marriage was held as late as is permitted and was followed by a great dinner/dance in a marquee. It was one of the wildest and wettest nights of the year and the marquees rattled and howled but the party was good. Later when Michael Langford had his 21st birthday party in the barn at Cold Nose on a fierce April evening I was reminded of Glen's wedding.

Early in 1975 John came back from the office one day with the prospect of becoming ambassador in Kabul. This pleased us very much. (Afghanistan was still peaceful) but it was not to be, luckily considering what happened there shortly afterwards, as about this time the office was also looking for a new Resident Commissioner for the Anglo-French Condominium of the New Hebrides and John with colonial experience and some passable French was an obvious choice. So at the end of July he found himself in Poitiers studying French intensively at the university there and staying with a French family. He used to drive off at lunch time in his little Mini estate and relax by the Vienne in order not to have to continue trying to think in French. I went to Cerbid with the children for the last time and when Peter and Richard were back at school, both at Shrewsbury now, and John's course was finished I flew by Dan Air to Tours where John met me and we then had a fine holiday in the Auvergne and from there drove by back roads to Bourges and so to Cherbourg. This holiday reawakened all my love for the French country side and for its history.

By now my mother was 75 and beginning to find Farmore and all it involved too much to look after, so after a certain amount of legal adjustment, we exchanged properties with her, she took Copper Beeches for £25,000, we paid her £25,000 and my marriage settlement had already given her a mortgage of £13,000 to help set up the Wye Valley Nursing Home. (She played a leading part in establishing this now flourishing Nuffield Hospital at a time when circumstances, both financial and political were not at all favourable towards private hospital care). So we got Farmore for £63,000 together with Cold Nose Farm, tenanted by Cliff Langford and the Lodge, occupied by Pauline Bell. Eventually we had to pay £1,800 in CTT but it was a good bargain. John left at the end of October for Vila to take up his new post and I remained to clear up Copper Beeches which my mother was going to alter and improve. I found this quite a painful process and the last evening in the nearly empty house felt rather desolate. (I had been very happy there.)

Towards the middle of November I left by Quantas for Sydney via Melbourne, First Class of course. Something went wrong with an engine so we were diverted to Amsterdam and spent some time on the ground there, drinking champagne and all becoming very jolly. A mistake, because by the time we reached Sydney where I was met by the British consul and taken to the Wentworth Hotel, I was completely exhausted and totally disoriented. The consul and his wife gave me a meal, I think I kept awake through it, but when Jean Champion, who was the the wife of John's cousin Phil, but has now died, came the next morning and very kindly showed me Sydney and took me to their house, I spent most of the time fighting off sleep and cannot have been a great credit to our side of the family. From Sydney I went by UTA to Noumea, spent a night there and flew on to Vila the following morning. By then my sleep pattern was readjusted but I was so little prepared for what awaited me that when I got off the little aircraft I was actually wearing stockings, which, I later learned, caused a great surprise to the welcoming group of John's colleagues and their wives.

31. New Hebrides
November 1975 — September 1976

The Anglo French Condominium of the New Hebrides as it was then, Vanuatu as it is now, is a group of largely volcanic islands lying south of the Equator between latitudes 13' and 21'. The islands are small, rocky, except for a few in the extreme north, forested and not heavily populated. It was Captain Cook in the 18th century who gave them their name as they reminded him, from the sea, of their Scottish fellows. During the winter (i.e. April — October) months when the weather is dominated by the S.E. Trade winds the climate is pleasant by day and almost cool by night on the other hand during the period November — March it is hot, humid, constantly raining and occasionally struck by cyclones. The indigenous population is largely Melanesian and is only beginning to recover now, in numbers and morale, from the traumas inflicted by the arrival of Europeans, that includes Americans, Australians and New Zealanders, in the 18th —

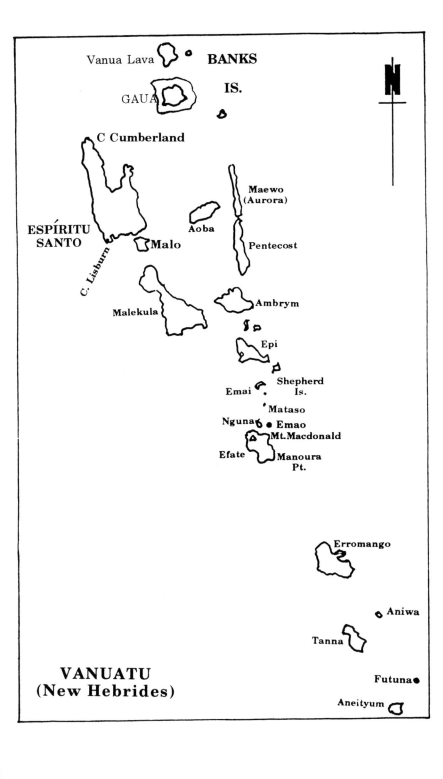

19th centuries. During that time imported diseases, especially measles, decimated whole communities, slavers, or black birders as they were called, lured young men with false contracts to work and die in the Queensland sugar plantations, and their traditional way of life, not I think particularly noble, was eroded by well intentioned missionaries. Since the 1939 — 1945 war, however, they have become part of the general Pacific cultural background and on the whole they have managed their independence very much better than many others elsewhere.

The Condominium was set up first in 1906 and developed further in 1914. The idea, thoroughly praiseworthy and prompted by the Entente Cordiale, was to prevent Anglo — French squabbles over territory and influence. However, the main effect of the system, which meant that nothing could be decided upon without joint agreement, resulted in it being difficult ever to get anything done at all. British and French District Agents busily intrigued against each other playing off the various tribal animosities encouraged by missionaries of varying creeds and I think I can say, with confidence, that after the three years I spent there I am sure that, whatever well meaning idealists may pretend, a Federal Europe will not work. That said however the French element was a great attraction in the life there, we made some good friends, there were excellent restaurants, the wine was good and above all Laurent Perrier champagne only cost 600ff. a bottle, cheap at the time.

The headquarters of the Condominium was at Vila (Port Vila to the French) on Efate island. The British Resident Commissioner lived in a modern white bungalow on Iririki Island about 400yds from the main island and about 40 acres in size. (I can understand the metric system; but I prefer to use the terms I was taught as a child). A smart little launch, the Nereid, transported us to and from the mainland and the crew lived down by the water's edge. Otherwise we and our staff were alone on our island perched on a cliff top approached by 177 steps, with a garden full of orchids and beautiful trees. Oranges, mandarins and limes grew wild, I have never tasted better, and we had a herd of cows led by a fine Charolais bull, Golden Boy, to keep the grass down.

British Residents's house on Iririki Island

Below the cliff on a level surface were the tumbling remains of the Paton Memorial Hospital, which had by now been resited on the main island. Paton had been a dauntless and courageous Scotch 19th century Presbyterian missionary. Our staff consisted of Silas Maqu' a portly Solomon Islander, his wife Helen, John, the head steward, Columbus his assistant and Kenneth who looked after the garden and the cows, all paid for by the Government. Maqu' was a person of authority and experience, he was also likeable and loyal. I don't forget coming back one night after being trapped on the other side by a minor cyclone and finding him and Helen, in their bathing suits, sweeping up water and broken glass in our living room. The French Resident Commissioner's much more luxurious house faced us from the mainland. The two flagpoles had been carefully theodolited so as to be exactly the same in height. There were, I think some 120 different tribal languages among the islanders and also a common pidgin called Bichelamar, evolved largely during the 19th century from contact with sailors, traders and missionaries. Here are two examples. A brassiere was "Basket blong titty"; 'My car has broken down completely,' "Truck blong me him bugger up finis". We got able to follow spoken pidgin to a certain extent but never learned to speak it ourselves although John did make prepared speeches in it. Each Resident Commissioner had his official touring boat. The French one, called *Armagnac*, was designed for the Mediterranean, it looked classy but couldn't cope with rough seas at all. Ours, *Euphrosyne II*, had been built in Australia at the same time as the Anglican bishop's touring boat and to the same design; but money had run short and the boat also was shortened so that it had rather a tub like appearance and rolled and tossed terribly; but was much more seaworthy than the French one. We had some good trips on the *Euphrosyne* and I came to like her and her Captain, Leif Nasak, who lived up to the very best seafaring tradition and would have done credit to the Blue Funnel Line, besides being very good company.

The process of settling into life in Vila was not easy. The climate was at its worst, it seemed to rain incessantly, there were mosquitoes and vicious biting flies and I felt at the end

Golden Boy

of the world, looking westwards into the rainy, setting sun I remember thinking that Ovid at Tomi can not have felt farther from home. Peter and Richard came out for the Xmas holidays and Pete looked up one day into the leaden, steaming sky and said somberly: "Who would think there could be so much water there?" However, we did our best to explore the island of Efate using the little second hand Mini-Moke John had bought for ourselves, the official car was an aged Jaguar. Richard took up shell collecting and we acquired a dug out canoe in which the boys paddled around. We also all swam off the harbour every evening and John and the boys snorkelled; but I noticed that some time later when an American film called "Jaws" was shown we all swam much less often, without saying anything about it however.

By April the weather had improved, John had started building our first boat, a Mirror called *Sabrina*, I had started riding at the Club Hippique introduced by Francoise Cazendres, wife of the French judge, and made twice weekly outings to canter through the coconut plantations and along forest paths on Benson, a little mare; we were getting to know people and beginning to feel more at home. William, who had left Oxford the year before with a 1st, came out for several months and came with us on trips in the *Euphrosyne* first to Malekula where Darvell Wilkins was British District Agent and kept a wonderful garden at Lakatoro and with his knowledge and experience was a stimulating and interesting guide. From Lakatoro we left in the *Euphrosyne* to sail south to round Malekula at night, and as the sky was lit by occasional fiery clouds from the volcano on Ambrym, I knew that I was glad to have come to the New Hebrides. Tanna was another island we visited, after first flying to Aneityum where William joined us on the *Euphrosyne* and from there, going by sea, to Futuna where the people were of mixed Polynesian descent and also to Aniwa and then to Tanna where Gordon Norris was BDA facing the formidable André Pouillet. Bob Paul, Australian settler and businessman was the uncrowned King of Tanna and he took us to see wild horses at Whitegrass, offspring of imported horses, running free in the bush, and also up to look into the volcano, rather disappointing I seem to remember. From Tanna we went to Erromango where we saw the graves of some 19th century missionaries killed by the locals because they had brought measles with them and so killed a large number of Erromangans, unintentionally of course.

Peter and Richard came out again at the end of July and Catherine, who was studying for her HND at Manchester had a free passage too. William went back to England shortly after to try for a PhD at Leicester. These holidays were thoroughly enjoyable, Catherine and I went often to the Club Hippique. John and I were by now sailing quite successfully in Sabrina and even winning, on handicap of course, races at the yacht club and the weather was good. I went with Catherine and the two boys on the *Euphrosyne* down to Tanna for a few days and stayed in Bob Paul's tourist bungalows. We saw the horses and the volcano but the trip was chiefly memorable for Richard being sick on the night passage down, 22 times. Catherine and I were feeling fairly poorly in the best cabin and I'm glad I didn't know till later that Richard was lying on deck among the local livestock being sick over the side. He was lucky not to go overboard. We came back by air.

Towards the end of September, after the family had left, John had to go to Paris and to London for official consultations. My mother had moved into Copper Beeches and David, who had gone to Lincoln with GEC but was not content there, decided to come to Farmore and to become what he has been ever since, the invaluable Warden. It seemed a good moment for us to move properly into Farmore so I followed John to London, flying by Nandi — Honolulu — Los Angeles, joined him in the flat, which badly needed cleaning, and after a visit to his parents, by now living in Chancellor House in Tunbridge Wells, went down to Farmore.

Euphrosyne

145

32. England and New Hebrides
September 1976 — October 1977

We arrived in England just after the record drought of summer 1976 and to compensate it rained steadily for about six weeks. John went back to Vila on September 22 while I stayed until November 12. I settled into Farmore, picked quantities of mushrooms, a vast crop was produced by the heavy rain following heat and drought, rode Goldie, started walking Ahu, planted bulbs and made a few trips to London. My Mother had improved Copper Beeches beyond recognition but the heart complaint that finally finished her was already beginning to be a trouble and she was restless and frustrated at not being able to do all she would have liked and very suspicious of interfering, well meaning advice. Fred Davies and two friends were doing a re-roofing at Farmore, much cheaper than a conventional builder, but there were certain disadvantages. One of the young men put his foot through a ceiling, and on one particularly wet and stormy night the polythene sheeting protecting Catherine's room blew off and rain came through down to the dining room. Catherine's room, now the spare room, has never quite got rid of the smell of damp carpet. However, all was made good and the roof 16 years later still holds.

Sally had gone to Canada in autumn 1974 to join Michael Murricane whom she had known at Bedales. She came home on holiday in October whilst I was still there, and stayed on over Christmas. She was working for the Canada Council, and had acquired quite a Canadian accent and also a very expensive black cat called Ricki whose later active and purposeful existence here, until the age of 16, was a credit to modern veterinary skills as, quite early in life, he had had, at the cost of several hundred dollars, some complex urinary operation which saved his life.

My journey back to Vila was made by Los Angeles and Fiji. The flight left Heathrow at about 1500 hours and flying north and west following the sun there was twilight from London until we were flying over the U.S. I had a window seat and it was eerie watching the setting sun for hours on end. Los Angeles airport was, as always, a confused muddle and my baggage got lost but reappeared a few days later at Vila. I found it easy to re-adjust to what was now a familiar way of life. John was occupied with the infinitely complex and frustrating process of trying to reconcile various political parties, commercial and business interests, French settlers, missionary influences, tribal and 'custom' factions such as Nagriamel led by Jimmy Stevens, and to persuade them to accept the need to move towards Independence in some form of order and all this in harmony with the French government. However, we found plenty of time for sailing and the usual round of sometimes rather bizarre parties.

We made a visit to Santo just before Christmas and were well cared for by Dick and Connie Baker, Dick was British District Agent there. Santo, or rather Luganville the town, was like a run down version of Jinja when we first knew it. We went to see a Japanese fishing enterprise and were taken round the sheds where huge fish, frozen solid were piled up like bombs. There was a fleet of Taiwanese fishing boats with large Gilbertese crews lolling around, playing cards and drinking. We visited Port Olry, a very beautiful bay with a mission station run by Père Limossier, a fanatical Frenchman with pale blue eyes, and after various other visits and 'Tok Tok' went back to the town in time for a great charity party given by the Kiwanis. I danced the Paso Doblo with Lefillatre the French District Agent, according to John Mme. Lefillatre was laughing helplessly.

Peter and Richard came out for Christmas and there were the usual activities, sailing, shell collecting and playing bridge, rather unpredictably, in the evenings. John was due for leave in the Spring; but there were various uncertainties about the date so I booked to go in early March. Before that we had a visit from Sir John and Lady Archer from Hong Kong who arrived in the middle of a storm by the same plane which took away Peter and Richard. Most of the Archer's visit was spent in buffetting wind and rain; but we had a party for them, the crossing to Iririki was only just possible, but all our guests arrived unharmed if dishevelled.

We made a tour of Maewo, Pentecost and Ambrym on the *Euphrosyne* at the end of January. On Maewo we saw a Gurkha detachment who were road building and also John presented a medal to Mark Meleu, a grand old patriarch and chief power in Maewo. After this we had to take part in some custom dancing — all the Gurkha officers were busy taking photographs; but we never got to see any, too ridiculous perhaps. When we went to land on Pentecost we were greeted by a political demonstration which was very neatly de-fused by Gerry Marsden (Darvell Wilkins' assistant who was with us); but our tour was clearly boycotted, rather conveniently as we were able to walk peacefully through the bush without any Tok Tok, Kai Kai or custom dancing. After visiting Ambrym we went over to Malekula and flew back to Vila from Lamap airfield. All our flights were made in little 12 seater Islanders; rather to my surprise, as I have always been a nervous flyer, I found I enjoyed these — it was satisfying to be able to look down and see land and sea beneath rather than clouds.

I flew back to England on March 11. Shortly afterwards Sally rang up from Canada to say that she and Michael Murricane were going to get married and would come home for the wedding which was to be in Dewsall church on May 28th. John came back on April 9th and the next few weeks were happy and busy with preparations for the wedding. But alas! it was not to be. Michael was killed in a car crash on the A49 early in the morning of the wedding. What followed was a nightmare. I will leave you to imagine it. Sally was immensely helped by the kindness of her friends, particularly Selina Cadell who was to have been bridesmaid and who went back to Canada with her afterwards to help clear up Michael's possessions and the remains of the joint lives. Ricki, the cat, was flown back to England and sent to quarantine for six months in Precious Pets' Valley in the Forest of Dean.

The rest of our leave was spent absorbing the shock and

trying to pick up the pieces. We all went out to Vila together, including Sally, at the end of July. John and I, paid for by the taxpayer, went First Class and Sally came with us, as a morale booster at her own expense, the others, also paid for by the taxpayer, were in Economy. It was daylight all the way to Los Angeles and from the plane there were wonderful, remote views of Baffin Island, the North West passage, broken ice flows, Hudson Bay and then northern Canada.

Once in Vila Sally was able to take up again her friendship with Dominique Burgess whom she had last seen in Uganda. Sandy Burgess was Chief Secretary when we first arrived and he and Josette had been immensely helpful while we were feeling our way in the curious world of the New Hebrides. Dominique and Sally went water skiing and to restaurants together and certainly this new/old friendship helped Sally to recover from her disaster. Later Dominique was to marry Bob Wilson who had been Assistant District Agent in Tanna, and they are now, 1993, in Hong Kong where Bob is a senior official, and they have four delightful children.

Catherine, Peter and Richard went back at the end of the holidays but Sally stayed on. It was decided that I should go back with her in the autumn and help her get started once more. We arranged for her to take over the flat in Redington Gardens and she was able to find work again at the Royal Opera House. However, before that she went with us on tour in the *Euphrosyne* to Tongariki,Tongoa, Epi and Emao. On Epi we joined Roby Gauger and other French for a joint ceremony followed by Kai Kai (food) and speeches. We then separated and from the *Euphrosyne* watched the *Armagnac* departing towards Valesedir submerged in spray. The passage to Emao was quite rough and John was horribly sick so much so that I was very impressed when on landing he managed an improving speech to as sullen a local council as I remember, urging them to cooperate with others and go forward together. A few years before a detachment of Gurkhas, paid for by the British taxpayer of course, had come to Emao and made a road round the island, to benefit the islanders. However, no one had made any attempt to maintain it and it was rapidly becoming overgrown. So we

149

left Emao with rather an unfavourable impression of its inhabitants.

Previously, in August, we had all taken part in the great Scout Walk. This was a sponsored walk of 25 miles round the east side of Efate in aid of the local scouts. John's predecessor, Roger du Boulay had done this, in record time, and we were not to be outdone, although John was not aiming to beat his record we reckoned that if the BRC's wife went too this would add another dimension. Catherine drove John, Sally and I out to Dry Creek in the Mini-Moke, Peter and Richard went out by bus together with Columbus young and fit. Pete had over ambitious plans to double the distance which in fact proved too much and he collapsed after 17 miles. The walk started at 7 p.m. so as to avoid the heat, and the early stages after Rentabao, walking along the shore to the sound of waves on the reef with the sky lit by a thin moon and occasional sheet lightning were romantic and beautiful. Catherine met us at 11 p.m. near the golf club bringing welcome soup and brandy and Sally, whose feet had become very sore, went back with her. But Gary Vandersluis, an Australian, had sponsored us, typically, for 5A$ a mile for the last five miles so we had to continue. It began to pour and then deluge as soon as Catherine and Sally left, with our anoraks, in the car. We were drenched, kept on stumbling into pools in the dark and for the last two miles I had to fight against an overwhelming desire just to sit down. However, we shuffled up the last hill to Tassiriki and arrived at the finish, soaked, exhausted but triumphant. We made 250A$ for the Scouts and got back to Iririki at 0245 next day.

I left Vila on 23rd October and Sally followed on the 29th. John was left alone to face 'Les Evénements', of which more later.

33. England — New Hebrides — England October 1977 – 1978

Back in England I was busy arranging the transfer of the London flat to Sally and with general activities at Farmore. Most important of these was having Ahu broken by Ann Hooley at Hoarwithy. We failed totally to get her into the horse box and Ann Hooley had to come with a lorry. Resolute blows with a yard brush drove Ahu in and she went off for a month. She came back well broken, always gentle but also always excitable and unpredictable. My mother was slowly but sadly deteriorating and refusing, determinedly, all well intentioned advice and assistance. I would too in similar circumstances so I sympathised, but worried about her. My brothers came several times to visit and at Christmas mother came to drinks and present giving but would not stay for the vast meal.

On November 29 I went down to Exmoor to stay with Charles and Diana Fulford Williams and while there heard and read of 'Les Evénements' in Vila. Reports in the press were confusing — I could not quite see how a crowd could have attacked our house on Iririki but later I realised that 'Residence' had been used instead of 'Residency'. It seemed that a crowd of 'Modérés', i.e. French supporters had attempted to attack the Vanuaku Party H.Q. and had been over enthusiastically sprayed with tear gas by Tim Osborne and Mike Dumper in charge of the British police. There was no sign of the French police, of course. After this the French crowd led by Rémy de la Veuve, Mayor of Vila, with tears streaming down his face, swarmed onto the British paddock and up to the Residency to be confronted by John feeling like Gordon at Khartoum. Fortunately they calmed down and Rémy was typically generous once he had recovered. There was a lot of trouble for John after this and Mike Dumper and Tim Osborne had to go. Curiously enough the French forgave John very much more thoroughly than the FCO officials did, and later, in August 1978, Dijoud, the French minister tried hard to persuade him not to leave but by then his departure was settled. In any case I think John has the distinction of being probably the only British official to have authorised the tear gassing of a French crowd. However I think it was lucky that he was awarded his well earned CMG before this happened.

When I went back to Vila at the end of January 1978 there had been several changes. Roby Gauger the FRC had left and gone to be a Sous Préfet in France. Whatever political differences he and John had had to contend with we had always liked both him and Colette and in the early '80s we had a very pleasant stay with them in Sarlat. Roby was replaced by 'Ce Jeune Pottier', an enarch and one time assistant to Olivier Stirn. His style was very different from the Gaugers' and parties at the French Residency were very much less well organised. John was as busy as ever with the immensely complex and frustrating negotiations towards achieving a satisfactory form for Independence but we still had time for sailing and a new and faster boat was built, a Miracle, called Galatea. We had some fairly impressive capsizes in Galatea before we learned to sail her successfully but eventually we were planing confidently and I learned how to sit on the side and lean out backwards in the approved manner.

Peter had left Shrewsbury at Christmas with a place at Balliol next autumn to read Arabic (this was not destined to be a success.) He came out to Vila early in February and stayed with us for several months; sailing (we bought him a Laser called Allegro ma non Troppo,) playing cricket (rather well) and joining a disreputable Australian sporting club called the Hash House Harriers. He made a great many friends and was pleasant company on Iririki. I went sailing with him several times, as crew, and was impressed by the quiet confidence with which he commanded his ageing mother sometimes in quite tricky situations. He spent 6 weeks hitch hiking and bussing round New Zealand during

152

their winter, visiting my Holt relations near Napier and also the Treadwells in Auckland who were very kind to him. He toured the South Island and returned to Vila in July, pale and with a cold, but unharmed despite being robbed in a Youth Hostel of most of his money.

John had applied to take early retirement when his tour in the New Hebrides came to an end and this had been agreed. So August was the last holidays. Richard came out and Catherine too, having successfully completed her HND. We had many rides together at the Club Hippique and she decided to stay on until we left and join us on the holiday we were planning in New Zealand. She also came with us on our two last tours on the *Euphrosyne*. The first to Tanna might well have had very nasty consequences for us all. Gordon Norris had been replaced as BDA by a New Hebridean, Job Dalesa, and he and his wife laid on a very fine supper for us, starting with crayfish. We were quite unaware of the extent of Catherine's allergy to shell fish so when she said she wasn't feeling very well we made light of it, not wishing to upset our hosts, and afterwards all went out leaving Catherine alone to lie down. She just didn't suffocate and was over the worst by the time we came back; but when we realised how nearly she had died we had a very thankful sensation of relief. The last tour of all was to the west coast of Santo and then up to the Torres Islands and on to the Banks and round back by Maewo and Aoba. So during our time there we saw all the New Hebridean islands including Reef Island, small and the only lagoon type island in the group. At Lolowai on Aoba there was a farewell party for us given by Bishop Rawcliffe, starting with a service in the Anglican cathedral, a building rather like a large cattle shed. This was enlivened by the intrusion of a bitch on heat pursued by randy dogs running round the legs of the officiating clergy. Derek Rawcliffe pretended not to notice and so did we, kneeling in the front row, but finally one of the junior acolytes administered a savage kick and they went elsewhere.

When we got back to Vila we started on a round of packing and farewell parties. Andrew Stuart, whom we had known in Uganda, was going to replace John as BRC and he and Pat and some family had paid us a visit in August to see what to expect. We sold our boats to them. The Mini Moke had been run into the back of a lorry outside Burns Philip by Peter a few weeks before and was done for. On October 21st I was rung up from England by Stopford to say that Mother was seriously ill in the Nuffield and I knew that I must go back. So, sadly leaving John and Catherine to say 'Goodbye' and have four happy weeks in New Zealand, I flew home on the 22nd.

I visited Mother in the Nuffield and was told by John Ross that her heart was only 50% effective so it was no surprise that when she came back to Copper Beeches, after a few attempts to get back to normal, she took permanently to bed and died, peacefully, early on November 21st.

34. December 1978 — August 1993
Yet Another Country

John and Catherine came back from a very successful holiday in New Zealand at the end of November and early in December there was a memorial service for my mother in Dewsall church. There was a great family gathering here, in Farmore, for tea afterwards.

Winter 1978 — 1979 was the first of the three cold winters there have been since we started living permanently in England and it was quite a change from Vila. I acquired a supply of thermal underwear and learned all the pleasures of cracked finger ends. Coming to live in Herefordshire was in many ways rather like settling into a new foreign posting. It was surprising to find how many of the old social and class distinctions still survived and were taken for granted especially after becoming accustomed to relaxed Antipodean Pacific attitudes. For instance we had become used to calling and being called by Christian names so when I joined our local Women's Institute and everyone was either Mrs or Miss it took me a long time to learn first names, some I never did. And it was a change to go out to black tie dinners after the parties in Vila where men wore embroidered Polynesian shirts and slacks and the women long Polynesian robes. But we enjoyed it from the first and I can say with certainty that for both John and I our 60s have been among the best years of our lives.

Douglas Chandler early recruited John as a St. John Ambulance President which led to him becoming St. John representative on the Regional Health Authority and then, from 1982 – 1986, the Chairman of the Herefordshire Health Authority. This brought him a great deal of interest, hard work, problems, new friendships and a small honorarium. After 1986 he became Chairman of the Appeal for Hereford cathedral and then Chairman of the cathedral Friends. This was a rewarding and fulfilling introduction to a new world, remarkably like Barchester in many ways, it was interesting to see it all in a late 20th century context. John's other ecclesiastical activity was as churchwarden of Dewsall and as organist of Dewsall and Callow. This was something he greatly enjoyed especially at Christmas — there were occasions when he was practising carols when I thought that if I heard 'Once in Royal David's City' once more I would scream but I managed to restrain myself. Playing the organ stimulated his musical talent and he studied harmony with Joan Spenser and also took and passed very well an O.U. course in music.

Then there was the RNCB of which he became a governor and later Vice Chairman. I very much enjoyed the RNCB connection particularly the Speech Days which took place in almost unfailing fine weather and were memorable for the most magnificent lunch for several hundred people produced by the head catering manager, Rachel. So sure was I of the weather for Speech Days that I could rely on the date each year for hay cutting and making.

We have five acres of land at Farmore and in addition to keeping up the garden, not up to the glories of my mother's time, but quite adequately for village fetes and parties, we have six sheep or so and during the spring/summer months

155

Farmore

however many lambs they succeed in producing. There are also assorted poultry and, of course, a horse, first Ahu and now an ageing grey poney, Dina. As Catherine said when I had a bad fall off Ahu two years ago and was considering a new horse, "You've got to be realistic about your age, Mother", so I try to be. Fred Davies, who went to work for Wiggins when Mother died, has now retired and comes to us twice a week. The results are remarkable, he is one of the world's great workers.

We found many other local interests, including the Woolhope Club with whom we made many enjoyable summer outings and attended some great winter lectures, notably by Jim Tonkin. However, one of the best sources of pleasure, interest and friendship has been the Cambrian Archaeoligical Association. Diana Currie introduced us to them in 1979 and we rapidly became enthusiastic and devoted Cambrians in spite of our Saesneg origins. John was the

Chairman of committees towards the end of this time and I would go with him to Aberystwyth for meetings, stay at magical Bronllolwyn by kindness of Denys and Dorothy Evans, spend a day exploring central Wales, and then while John was at the committee meeting, walk along the seafront and up on to the cliffs and along the coastal path. One of the great attractions of the Cambrians, apart from the knowledge and the interest provided by their meetings, has been the pleasure of congenial company. You can do exactly as you like, there are plenty of opportunities for talk and whisky drinking; but you can go off on your own if you like without feeling pressurised.

As well as life in Herefordshire there have been our journeys abroad. Between 1980 and 1991 we made four trekking tours in the West Himalaya, around Manali, crossing the Rohtang three times into Lahoul, and crossing passes of 14,000 and twice 16,000ft and getting to know something of the local people, and also seeing Manali becoming swamped by tourism so that I have now no wish to go again. We also went to Nepal in 1982 when Jenny Hobbs was with the British Council there and spent a wonderful month in October staying with her in Kathmandu, trekking from Gorkha to Pokhara, and then exploring Kathmandu and Bakhtipur by foot and bus. Once we went on a round world trip starting with Vancouver Island where we stayed with Ron and Peggy Harvie, old Uganda friends, and then going on to New Zealand — Australia and so home, this took about six weeks from late October till mid December. We went in 1989 to New Zealand again and explored both islands with a hired car staying in motels and visiting the less touristy parts. I love New Zealand — if I were young now I would find a way to live there by any means, there is space and there are still some wild places.

During the intervening years we would go the France, staying in self-catering gites hired through VFB. These have always proved most successful giving us complete independence and all basic necessities. We have been twice to the Pyrenees, twice to the Alps, twice to the Cevennes and once to the Jura. Also we went to Scotland, to Skye in 1979 and then in 1990 to the Outer Hebrides taking the car by ferry between the islands and experiencing a good variety of weather from a blue and brilliant afternoon to savage horizontal rain the following morning. So we have benefited to the full from good health and good fortune during the last years.

In October 1990 we had an unusual and exciting holiday. We crossed the Channel by Hovercraft and then went from Boulogne to Paris by rail and from there by night train to Venice where we spent three nights in perfect autumn weather staying by the lagoon in the house where Vivaldi had lived at one time now the Metropole Hotel. We visited churches and museums and art galleries, walked along beside the canals, made a boat trip to the outer islands and went to a concert in the church where Vivaldi's orphaned girls choir had sung. Venice was as beautiful as a painting by Canaletto and there were not too many other people. From Venice we went by train to Ljubljana, not to be recommended, that is the train journey, where we were thankful to be met by Jenny Hobbs who was then head of the British Council office in Zagreb. With her we saw some beautiful parts of Slovenia, again in lovely weather, and had a very interesting fortnight in Zagreb. Yugoslavia was just starting to disintegrate and we were left in no doubt of the feelings of the Croats towards the Serbs, nor of the righteousness of their cause, so easy is it to identify with other people's prejudices if you find them personally congenial and know nothing of the other side of the case.

Various family changes have also taken place. In one direction several of us have gone. John's father died in 1982, while we were in Nepal, at the age of 88. His end was like my father's swift and worthy. John's mother died in January 1990, shortly before her 97th birthday. Her last years were not too happy as she was increasingly helpless in a nursing home but her mind and her wit remained with her to the end. And, sadly, my brother Stopford died comparatively young, in 1986. In the other direction Richard and Donna, who married in 1986, have Hamish and Isabelle and now Alfred to go forward, Lawrence and Heather have Nicholas and Joanna, and Catherine, who married John Emberson in 1987, has Robert and Charles to carry on, I hope, their parents good qualities.

158

In September 1992 we went to Eisenstadt and Linz with a Martin Randall tour, very well organised and ably and wittily led by John Savory Harrison, himself a musician and half Austrian. The weather was good, the country beautiful, the music varied and exciting and the visits to abbeys, churches, palaces and towns a reminder of what there remains to be seen and enjoyed of the old Habsburg civilization. It was one of our best holidays and I hope to go with Martin Randall again. At the beginning of October we went for a weekeend with the Cambrians to Oswestry. Here the weather was less kind, stormy with a cold wind, but again it was the Cambrians at their best. On October 20th I went into the Nuffield to have a troublesome bunion on my left foot removed by Ian Reynolds. The operation has been a great success and now I am hardly aware of it. At the beginning of November John went up to London to attend the 7th Armoured Division's Alamein dinner and it was while tying his bow tie then that he noticed the first symptoms of the malevolent disease which was to destroy him. Fortunately Creuzfeldt-Jakob's disease did not reveal the full extent of its malign powers until mid-December so he was able to see and enjoy the installation and dedication of Simon Beers beautiful Corona in Hereford cathedral, a project which had absorbed so much of his enthusiasm and given him so much pleasure and interest during the preceding 18 months.

Epilogue

When David and I brought John home from Birmingham, where CJD had been diagnosed, in January 1993 we were told he would not last more than six months from the first noticeable symptoms of the disease. That had been in November 1992 — now it is August 1993 and he is still with us, albeit only in a slowly but steadily shrinking bodily form and no longer as a person. We have been able to look after him at home, thanks to David without whose strength and thoughtfulness it would be impossible. I think it a privilege to be able to do this. Ours has been a good marriage; we have been friends of the best kind, sharing sufficient interests and companionship but making no excessive demands upon each other and I realise how fortunate I have been. Now I have to look forward to a future on my own; but still hope to reach A.D. 2,000 which appears to me rather like the cairn at the top of a hill.

Thinking of the year 2,000 brings with it thoughts on the human situation. It seems to me that during the last 200 years, and accelerating in the last 50, we humans have succeeded in changing our environment faster than we are biologically capable of adapting to it. And so the resulting pressures, social, political, economic, demographic and environmental are likely to prove more than we or our institutions can control and as a result the 21st century is likely to see change and disruption beyond our present comprehension. I wonder what sort of a world my grandchildren will inhabit. But I do not feel too concerned because if my grandmother, Olive Jacks whom I remember well, could have lived to see how, during the last 40 years, the ideals and standards, which she believed to be right, have been discarded and rejected, she would have sorrowed greatly, but I have had an interesting and rewarding life and I hope my grandchildren may have, in a different way, as good opportunities. And so I shall wish them good health, good luck, courage and a sense of humour. That should see them through whatever the 21st century has to offer.

Olive in 1993 with Tin Tin on the
Black Mountains in the rain...